Politicology
A Minor Genealogy of Power.

S.John

DEDICATION

For Sax, Silv and my perfect Emmy Lou.
I can do better. I will do better. I must do better.
All my love, always.

Philosophy is the practice of critical, interrogative thinking.

Ideology is a destination, to which philosophy is the journey.

This destination affects the entire trajectory of your life as an individual, and sometimes - just sometimes - the trajectory of the entire human race

Contents

ACKNOWLEDGMENTS

This, whatever "this" is, would not be possible without my family and my incredible network of support. In particular, Emmy Lou, without whom I would not be what I am today.

I
Introduction.

"The first question is not: what particular code of values should man accept? The first question is: Does man need values at all- and why?"- Ayn Rand

***

Life is a curious condition. Unlike writing, life has no second draft. Perhaps that is why all lives, in their own way, are the most beautiful disasters. This book, on the other hand, does have the luxury of the potential second chance. Thankful as I am for that ability, it doesn't actually seem to help all that much, and this has often made me wonder if the ability to have a second go at life would be that much of a useful option. In any case, this book has been a challenge to write because, at the core of it, the purpose is to ask questions. Now, questions are good in one sense, because they encourage you to look for answers. This does, however, present quite a unique problem, in so far as usually, it is only *good* questions that encourage the pursuit of useful answers; almost by definition. My intention here, considering this principle, is to ask or present "good" questions.

The art of good questioning is a difficult beast to tame, and asking questions (any questions) to yourself may or may not quickly illustrate why. For me, it is complicated because the messages contained within the following pages are, largely by design, not so precise. For this reason alone, I had to ask myself a serious question: what is the point of this book? An ironic question for a book centred in no small part around philosophy, I know, but life can be like that sometimes. It became apparent to me after much consideration that this book has one core intention: to expand the boundaries of thinking for anyone reading it, and to encourage them to consider- to think- beyond their usual intellectual limitations. It is a book written with an honest and hopefully naked agenda of both offering insights into certain phenomena and to encourage deep, unwelcome thinking. To inspire within the hungry mind that appetite for the flavour of philosophical exploration.

It is no secret that the 21st century has so far been postmodern to the core. It is no secret that truth is hard to find or even define in the post-fact world which we now inhabit. It is also no secret- and no small shame- that to the average person- the average *thinker*- the value of philosophy, understood as the deep, subjective consideration of ideas, has been diminished, in the behemoth shadow cast by the "observe, measure, repeat" scientific method; a method itself that is often fatally misunderstood.

As such, I would like to take this opportunity to suggest that this book is, in the rawest sense, a piece of philosophical interrogation. Science, or at least the pursuit of understanding through the strict scientific method, will not be the subject of this short book. That being said, our modern and arrogant expectation that perhaps the scientific method *should* be the only method of interrogation seriously practiced, perfectly exemplifies what is, because so much of our thinking now seemingly relies upon it. Accordingly, this book will seek to explore the ways in which philosophy is developed, its relationship with ideology, and how ideology impacts and influences the development of opinion, perception and ignorance. From there, it seeks to explore (by no means exhaustively) how these things translate into power, usually through the medium of politics. It seeks to explore the importance of philosophy and how it affects *everything* about our daily lives.

This book seeks to examine questions of what ideology is at its core, how it is developed and why it translates into actions, as well as how it manifests itself in politics. It seeks to ask questions, specifically, and to inspire critical thought surrounding the idea of ideology and our susceptibility (as a whole species) to intellectual manipulation and misinformation. In this account, I use the tools at my disposal, where possible, to explore the concepts within, and provide, amongst other things, what I hope is a raw window into my political development, as an infamous "millennial" forced to navigate the world as it has become. And my position as a millennial is not inconsequential; we as a generation have seen perhaps the largest paradigm shift in human existence since the discovery of fire. The laptop I am writing this on and the phone in my pocket should largely indicate as to why.

The power of thinking has been heavily diminished and oversimplified i the 21st century, which is perhaps a curious thing to say given what we know about the world in which we now live. We have unprecedented access to information, unprecedented access to education, unprecedented governmental transparency (at least in the West) and the world is functionally smaller than it has ever been. As such, entertaining the idea that our ability to think- to philosophically consider- has collapsed knowing all of this may seem counter-intuitive. All the symptoms are easily visible though, like for example that whenever arguments ensue online "facts" are thrown around like snowballs as though those who threw them made the snow. Every answer to any question we might have is at the click of a button now. Some call this progress, but it looks a lot to me like regression; google has done to the intellect what spellcheck has done to grammar. It has rendered us helpless, lazy and reliant on a false God. It has rendered us intellectually placid.

That which used to be sacred to the art of becoming enlightened- study, research, reading, understanding, discussion with peers and argument with those who disagree- has been bastardised, and half-hearted versions of all those things seem to plague us all now. The advent of technology has not been, sadly, the advent of universal enlightenment. Quite the opposite, in fact, and we may well be on the cusp of another half millennium- long dark age. Regardless, I won't be here to see it even if we are. But I am here to bear witness to the beginnings of what will certainly be a tumultuous journey on the road which leads to human integration with technology.

That road, however, is only partially the concern of this book (although it is a huge area of philosophical potential going forward). This book will be more looking to explore how and why we, in an age of unprecedented access to information, still offer so little critical thought to the concepts of ideology, philosophy and power. It will be looking to explore what those concepts are, and how they are implemented and utilised. It will be looking to inspire within the reader some semblance of thinking beyond the narrow self.

As such, there will be a notable lack of convention throughout. This is partly due to a fatigue within the author of adhering to convention in everything he does, only to be rewarded with nothing but the sound sleep afforded by a life of uneventful uniformity. For this reason, there will be, amongst other things, a notable lack of academic referencing. Referencing in the postmodern era demonstrates little more than proficiency with internet search engines. I don't subscribe to the pseudo- intellectual culture we have cultivated that puts so much blind faith in established norms, as though the norms themselves didn't take any normalising, and axioms of etiquette were always axiomatic. More than that, I am fundamentally hostile to the idea that an opinion, as analysis and commentary of this sort is, is confirmed or propped up by hollow, often highly laboured and arbitrary reference substantiation. In many ways, that is the *point* of the whole piece. There is, however, a further reading section at the end should your curiosity best you.

To appropriate the sentiments of Nietzsche, the tree loses no sleep considering whether or not you will enjoy its fruits. It simply offers them, and their inherit nutritional value, with an open and exposed honesty. To exemplify my sentiment here, does the last paragraph sound arrogant? If so, is that a problem? *Why* is that a problem? What in particular is wrong with arrogant delivery, and why does it detract from the usefulness of what is being said? Questioning is good; questioning allows for the mind to free itself from the shackles of convention. Questioning allows the mind to explore meaning, and realise that meaning is not rigid.

What *is* the point, then, I hear you so philosophically enquire? Well, the goal is simple: to give at the very least a benchmark from which to enquire deeper into the subjects covered in this short book. To encourage and remind us that all thought is not yet thunk, that all considerations are not yet considered, that all evidence is not yet evidenced, and that the beautiful, artful process of philosophy is not, for humanity, an as yet completed task. To me, all of these issues are being forgotten in the dogmatic grey imposed by the "observe, measure and repeat" scientific method which has been championed by western society in the 21st century hitherto. Ironic that it is precisely this dogma and scientific fetishism that ushered in the postmodernism of flat earthers and gender choosers, with all their seemingly unlimited and unrelenting hypocritical arguments shrouded in a veneer of that which is often only just observable, seldom measurable and only disingenuously repeatable.

This book is not written to be a text of ultimate and/ or absolute authority, it is written with the virtuous intention of encouraging you, the reader, into further enquiry of the subjects covered within, and perhaps to encourage an alternate and different perspective; to encourage the pursuit of understanding and to encourage deeper critical thinking. To empower your mind, even just a little bit, with accessible and concisely digestible theories, questions and propositions. To inspire the smouldering embers of a prospective 21st century philosopher to develop into a freshly emancipated roaring inferno of thought and consideration. To remove the shackles of the 21st century mind from the snake oil of scientific dogmatism (though not to challenge the notion of science as we know it, nor to challenge its supreme and bona fide usefulness- just to challenge its seeming universal superiority over other methods of data collection, social commentary and consideration). Remember, for all the questions science has guided us towards an answer to, we still have no definitive answer to such seemingly basic questions like "what is morality?", "what is virtue?", "what is the mind?" and even, "is reality real?". Rene Descartes probably still takes the crown for 'best rationalist answer'.

To me, the era within which we currently live will surely be one of the most intriguing throughout all of human history, from our conception to our inevitable (probably self) destruction. We live in an unprecedented era of postmodernism, of inaccessible truth, and diversity of ideology. We live in a world of conflicting ideas, a world of repetitive social issues, and uniquely venomous politics. We live in a world of simultaneous information saturation and universal ignorance. We live in a world of brilliance and stupidity, potent policy and violent confrontation. We live in a world of terror, manipulation, power struggles and philosophy.

It is a beautiful and extraordinarily dangerous place to be.

II
The Honesty of Ignorance.

"Man is born free, but everywhere he is in chains" – Jean-Jacques Rousseau.

Education is critical to our development- not just intellectually, but philosophically. As soon as we can comprehend the idea of 'speciality disciplines', or even comprehend 'words' and 'meaning' in general, we in the UK (and most of the western world) are taught and exposed to at least three core subjects: mathematics, English and science. We get a little older, and subjects like art become fairly standard. Move on just a couple more years and we are learning history, I.T, and religious education. Edge us up into the twilight of our primary school tenure and we have things like geography, music and drama. The order may be a little bit askew, but the point withstands that margin of error: all the above are things that by the time we get to high school, we have *some* understanding of, past that of basic subject definition.

Upon arriving at high school, as an eager, fresh faced eleven year old, we are thrust into more of a dynamic educational atmosphere, with set timetables, new subject disciplines such as a second or third language, the splitting of science into the three disciplines of biology, chemistry and physics, the introduction of CAD and CAM into our basic technological understanding, and the dreaded introduction to the mathematics of Pythagoras. Interestingly,

Pythagoras perhaps perfectly illustrates the sentiment of this chapter, insofar as many people recognise and even understand the classic $a^2+b^2 = c^2$ equation, but very, very few people know of Pythagoras as an ancient philosopher, let alone his rudimentary theory of forms, allegedly influencing the works of Plato and as such having a key role in the development of thought and understanding as we know it today.

We are never really given the option to study philosophy, the foundations of ideology or even politics until at best the very end of our school premiership- the last couple of years- and even then, we are never encouraged to think for ourselves about theories, the intricacies of ideology or the process of philosophy. We are never introduced to metaphysics or metaethics, at least in the same way we are introduced to complex and difficult sciences, and we are exposed to the small amounts of political ideology and theory that we *are* exposed to through the intellectual prisms of thought that are our teachers[1]; a point that is of *profound* importance.

The teacher in many ways is as important as the subject. As a society, we are against things like creationists teaching science because quite obviously it stands to reason that their teachings will inevitably be subjective, erroneous and damaging to the education of our children. We are, however, generally (and unfortunately) ignorant to this principle beyond relatable and clear-cut examples. The reasoning behind why most of us wouldn't want a creationist teaching science is hopefully obvious; primarily it is because of the intrinsic bias and limited intellectual potential for the teachings of the creationist to convey the subject of science.

There is an implication here: if we know who we wouldn't want to teach our kids science, then it stands to reason that we ought to know who we *would* want teaching them science; someone with a degree in the subject, and if possible, experience in their field, right? This same discussion holds perversely true for how we are taught politics, albeit the answers to those questions in the context of politics have a much more broadly damaging scope. It is also worth remembering that politics is never *explicitly or formally* taught to most children at least until around age 14, but is absolutely present in their education, as is philosophy and ideology; these things are present in every and all interactions the child- the student- is involved in, and all these things shape everything from their global outlook to their morality.

---

[1] Understood not just as professional educators, but as *all those* who teach us throughout childhood; all those from whom we learn *something*.

At this point, we should extrapolate our logic a bit further. Who, for example, would we want overtly teaching our children morality? Your preference here is likely to depend in large part upon *your* political beliefs, not the qualifications of the teacher; what *you* would have not just your child, but *all* children taught, in terms of ideology, politics and philosophy, in schools. For example, would you rather a Nazi with a political science Ph.D. or a neoliberal with a third-class bachelor's degree be responsible for teaching philosophy and morality? The same question should be asked about who we might want to teach these things covertly, and it ought to be a concern of deep consideration, too.

Unfortunately (or potentially not so unfortunately) it isn't up to you, and what is *actually* taught regarding these things in the classroom is in fact entirely up to the teacher. Not just in terms of the curriculum[2] being followed and delivered, but the *actual, true content* involved in the process of *teaching*. Everything from the nuanced, intended meaning behind the words spoken, to the teacher's choice of examples in explanations; one's choice of language often highlights one's own internal, inescapable biases, sometimes woefully referred to in the modern landscape as 'unconscious bias'. When "one" is a teacher (or, more widely, any authority figure), those biases have the potential for extreme intellectual consequence.

It is a seldom critiqued reality of any curriculum, in life as well as education, that they completely ignore the fact that in *any area*, true objectivity is extremely difficult (if not impossible) to achieve, and it is abjectly wrong to assume, as the objectivist might do, that there is a "neutral" or self-evident default position; everything is predicated on *a priori* assumption. Every concept is understood with language as a result of experiential exposure: in the immortal sentiment of Wittgenstein, we don't understand until we learn how to describe. Does everyone want equality of the sexes, for example? Firstly, define "equality". Secondly, apply it to everything; does a 50/50 gender split make everything better? Does it truly improve the world? Even if it doesn't, perhaps people *should* want that, as far as *you're* concerned, but demonstrably not *everyone* does. Are those who don't want it right, or are they wrong? Is their opinion true to themselves and if it isn't, are they wilfully living a lie? IF we can suggest their opinions are wrong, can't we identify the possibility that actually, it is *your* opinion that is wrong? There are no simple answers to these questions

---

2 the formal content of the lessons, again understanding that lessons in life also have a curriculum.

at all, but the consequences of presuming the answers are simple and easy are wildly detrimental, and everywhere to see.

This is because objectivity within politics, ideology and philosophy simply does not exist- objectivity as a concept, perhaps to its very core, barely exists at all (if at all)[3]. The act of describing something in a certain way, your method of teaching, the decisions you make as to who you speak to and don't- every choice you make, every decision you make- is you exhibiting *some* subjective bias in *some way*. Your favourite colour is a bias. Your favoutite brand of footwear is a bias; the very act of having *favourites* is the act of expressing bias. Crucially, so too is the act of choosing how you describe concepts and things, down to the precise choice of words you use, or even more damningly the lazy choice of words you use; the precise omission of words you do not use. In the case of the teacher[4] specifically, these biases profoundly affect how they *teach*.

Education.

Throughout childhood, and into adolescence, we *usually have* zero *academic* influence on our understanding and grasp of either the concepts or disciplines of philosophy, ideology and politics. How then, might we shape our world view? Well, I simply can't (and wouldn't even try to) speak for everyone- naturally, as we are all different. I can, however, for the sake of establishing an intellectual foundation upon which to build, cast my mind back to when I was in school a mere decade or so ago. In fact, I can literally cast my mind back to the very incident that shaped my political and philosophical outlook as it is today; though, that will come later. For now, the influences I specifically remember as a child, a teenager, a waster at college and finally, an undergraduate.

When I was a child, I went to a Church of England primary school. The kids used to tell risqué and sometimes even racist jokes every now and again, that they didn't really understand. I distinctly remember being perplexed as to why they would tell these jokes that were so far beyond their understanding,

---

[3] As explained and explored by Ludwig Wittgenstein in his superb polemic *"Tractatus Logico- Philosophicus"*- principally visible in the exploration of the idea that a picture represents an objective truth but our attempts to articulate the same picture being inhibited, naturally, by our language limitations.
[4] Remember our definition of "teacher" is not strictly academic; it is reference to anyone who teaches you anything.

and disheartened that I was supposed to laugh but didn't really know why. In fact, I thought they were wrong; not formally incorrect, but *morally* wrong. For you see, this school (like all schools) taught us that racism was bad. Full stop, bad. Similarly, my parents also taught me that racism was bad. Full stop. It was established very early on as the consensus from all dimensions of authority in my life.

The problem for me was that none of these figures of authority ever taught us why. To be honest, that's fairly reasonable considering we were kids and the now obvious complexity of doing so, but oblivious as I then was, I always found my infant-self wondering: *why?* In the same way my feelings towards the jokes were bemusement and confusion, based on the fact that these kids were just saying something for the sake of saying it with no understanding, so too did my philosophical interrogation manifest itself in intrigue and scepticism; I didn't find these jokes particularly funny, but why were they wrong? *Why* shouldn't I be racist? Why shouldn't I be *anything* for that matter, so long as I could find reason (not necessarily *good* reason) for doing so? A good question for philosophical scrutiny or exploration, and yet no opportunity for scrutiny or exploration was provided. A time when the human mind is at its most free, most naked, most hungry, and no one was there to feed it- It seemed like everyone was simply there to *fill* it.

As Great British protocol had it, my SATS came and went, and, in mid-August of 2003 I got to high school. Boy, if primary school was a sensory lake then high school was an ocean. Highschool continued the trend against racism and very quickly partnered it with another clear trend: bullying. Bullying was met with severe punishment in high school (not least because bigger students had the potential for greater violence), and this punishment was only paralleled with that given to anyone guilty of racism. On top of that, there were even posters in some of the classrooms in high school of a variety of brains- male, female, black, white etc- with that of a racist in the bottom corner represented as a quarter of the size of the others; the racists were even being openly mocked. These things- bullying and racism- were bad, but they weren't morally or philosophically bad, they were presented as objectively *bad*, axiomatically wrong. And they were always punishable offences. In that respect, we were *told* what was right and wrong, *told* what to do and not do, how to be and not be. The wrongness of these things was approached as self-evident, axiomatic and *a priori- they were* wrong simply because they were wrong. The foundations of our thinking were being covertly laid *for* us, not *by* us.

These points were then politicised. For example, there were discussions between teachers as to the incompetence of the Tories, how terrible Margaret Thatcher's *bullying* of the miners was. In an attempt to befriend some of my revered educators, I supposed (as did some of my friends) to adopt this narrative and its sentiment. We spoke about how Thatcher *bullied* the miners and the unions, how she and her party were *racist,* and only *for the rich.* Since I had been conditioned to hate bullying and racism, and I didn't see myself as even remotely wealthy, the Tories, it seemed fair to conclude, were not the party for me. In other words, I was conditioned against right-wing ideology and philosophy before I could even *comprehend* what it was, or give an example of a single right-wing thinker. Thatcher included- I was ignorant to definition or faction alliance, as were all of my friends in school at that same point. And with great surety, I do say and mean, *all.* This is not to say, to be clear, that firstly either bullying nor racism are at all conditions of conservative or Tory thinking, nor secondly to suggest the teachers did this with any specific malice in their hearts; just to illustrate how the journey of ideological realisation can be one wrought with a spectrum of ignorance.

Content with this ignorance for the time being (as kids usually are), with no education on the subject whatsoever and just based around my school life and the discourse that filled it, I assimilated myself, around year 9 (or third year for those vintage readers out there) as an ardent Labour supporter. I was red. I remember saying silly things, soundbites of what I thought were supreme intellectual ramblings that I didn't really understand, and a slightly younger me would have been confused to hear me say, such as that infamous, ludicrous idiom: "communism is a good idea, but it would never realistically work in practice". I didn't even know what communism was, let alone why the hell Karl Marx was important to it. But I was never challenged by any authority figure - I wasn't told that I was necessarily right, but I certainly wasn't told that I was wrong, in the same way that the racist or the bully was told they were wrong and in any case, there was no theatre in which to pose those opinions for open discussion anyway. Thusly, I took every opportunity to swim well beyond my depth in the pool of political discussion and social commentary available to me at school. My canny angle in school was to befriend as many teachers and figures of authority as possible, and adult conversation was my perceived key to that door. And then, one summers evening on the drive home from school- probably around late June- I was talking to my mum in the car, about politics and my newfound grandeur of opinion on the subject.

I was asking her how she was going to vote in the coming election, and why. She said that it was personal, so I suggested things about the Labour government that I liked, as well as my unrelenting disdain for Thatcher. My mum asked me why I thought Thatcher was bad, and all I could say was (literally in list form) miners, milk and poll tax. She asked me what else I knew, and I couldn't answer, to which my mum told me that Thatcher wouldn't have been as popular as she was, had she been no good. This was interesting to me, as a person to whom I gave my absolute and highest level of trust and faith was presenting to me an opinion to which I had been little if ever exposed to that point, and planting the seed that was to blossom into an insatiable curiosity: the idea that there is always more to know than you are told.

Into the twilight of my high school tenure and the blossoming of my college experience, I did some reading, some more investigation, and some more research. I also had that little snippet echoing constantly in my head: there is always more to know than you are told. It got me thinking, that perhaps there is more to what you see than you are shown, that maybe this political opinion was shaped not by simply these explicit political conversations, but my entire experience with education. As such I started listening and watching much, much more. The revelations were startling.

All of my teachers were in unions. Many of the kids I went to school with had parents that were unemployed and on some iteration of social welfare. Labour, within both of those demographics, were (and still are) obscenely popular; more than that, the Conservatives were obscenely *unpopular,* and it became pretty apparent to me that narratives are shaped just as much- if not more- by the unpopular than they are by the popular.

A broad political narrative began to take shape, the essence of which being that bad things happen and the Conservatives either caused them or would make them worse. Conservative voters were always characterised as selfish (undesirable quality) and rich (does not apply to me). In college, I was taught by a Liberal Democrat activist, Labour supporters and union members. In university, I was lectured by two Labour councillors, a woman married to one of them, a Liberal Democrat supporter and a Marxist author. I was criticized openly not for expressing right leaning opinions; not objectively incorrect, or even irrelevant or irreverent views, but for expressing right-wing views. I was criticized explicitly for them being right-wing; the actual wording on one assignment was "Faragist".

From start to finish, thought throughout my education was always imposed, never inspired, let alone encouraged, even (depressingly) in university, where lecturers would read blocks and blocks of notes from pre-prepared power points, and essentially drill into you what you *'needed'* to know in order to pass the papers and exams. Thought was imposed, rendering thinking-philosophising- difficult and for the most part, useless. Certain ideas were relevant, certain ideas were not; you were essentially told what you needed to know. It's interesting, the notion of being told what you *need* to know; you're literally being told that you are about to receive an explicit agenda of thought, a collection of information that certain minds have deduced as useful, and that you should by proxy accept that information as unquestionably valuable.

Aside from studying History and Politics at university, where independent thought was a struggle but at a push (and oftentimes incurring negative consequence) *could* be achieved, my education- and importantly, British education in general- consisted of sub-basic philosophy and political theory, and was at the mercy of nothing but the behest of those teachers so bold as to overtly explain their agenda as political. Other than that, they- political ideology, philosophical education and theoretical discussion- disappeared into background noise. They were hidden by the mistress of subtlety.

This phenomenon is one that all the evidence available to me, in my experience as both a student and a lecturer in the further education (FE) and higher education (HE) sectors, suggests is persisting. Students are coming out of education with little to no knowledge of philosophy, political ideology, or even the ceremony of politics other than the soundbites they have been conditioned into accepting, which are almost always iterations of left-wing doctrine. Students are protesting things they don't understand, and don't even know of, based on the fact their educator engendered sensibility sees it as conducive behaviour. There were some brilliant examples of this at the march against hate in Manchester on the 11th June 2017, the sporadic 'extinction rebellion' protests or the anti-Donald Trump mavericks demonstrating little more than the lacking extent of the student political education. They are there because of what they have been *told,* a mistake the writings of Immanuel Kant[5] amongst others persuade us to avoid, a lesson these people undoubtedly missed precisely because of the lacking philosophical education in Britain today.

Media and Echo Chambers.

After education, we have what is certainly a contender for first place but probably on balance the second biggest ideological influence in a 21st century young person's life after their peers: media. Media comes from many places and is available in many mediums, aided in no small part by the coming

---

5 Most famously in his polemic letter *"What is Enlightenment"* written in response to a question raised by Reverend Johann Friedrich Zöllneron on the notion of marriage outside of the church and published in the December 1784 issue of the Berlinische Monatsschrift (Berlin Monthly).

of the internet, and perhaps the most influential of all these avenues and mediums, and the one which commands the majority of our attention, has become social media.

The influence of social media has been profound. There have been many major intellectual fallouts from this social media explosion, ranging from the curious Trumpian phenomenon of "fake news" to the establishment of social media companies as the great pretenders to the throne of censorship with things like de-platforming and global speech regulation. Social media also seems to be making people *en masse* more ignorant and in general, bigoted. In many ways social media is a perfect storm for harbouring ignorance; we would rarely if ever go on Facebook for a relaxing night of browsing and content consumption with the direct intention of becoming educated, in the same way we might expect and intend when stepping into a lecture theatre. As such one's mind is entering that world from a position of limitation, and is likely to be nowhere near as open as it would be in a lecture theatre (and even there, most minds are not as open as they ought to be) because the intention is nowhere near as focused.

But that is not to say that there is nothing to learn from social media, or that social media isn't constantly teaching whether we pay attention or not. Social media has a lot to teach us regardless of whether we have the intention of learning. What constitutes a "community standard", for one; a lesson most social media users learn at some point or another as they cross that blurred line between acceptable and unacceptable per the sensibilities of the billionaire majority shareholder at the top. This particular example is a lesson in politics, and an exercise in conditioning. It is also the demonstration of a supreme power that no global entity ought to possess; the ability to make a captive audience of billions police themselves to abide by the standards of whichever demigod sits in the chair of the relative CEO. Such has been the development of the online world and social media that a select few intellectual oligarchs do, sadly possess this power.

Another curiosity of the social media influence on our philosophical and political development is the idea that what we see on social media depends entirely upon *where we look*, and oftentimes this principle (as transparent as it is) is the basis of how content creators produce what they produce as they jostle and fight for what little attention we have to give. Our attention is regularly captured by subtleties; we are snared by the subliminal. Perhaps the most obvious demonstration of all these concepts is the unique propensity of news pages to show tiny snippets of information, taking advantage of the fact that they know that their audience is in an environment where they are almost naturally inclined to trust them; things like showing a headline and a caption with no compelling reason to read the full article, for example.

Oftentimes, when we see these headlines and captions an unconscious conditioning of bias is trickled into our *passive* thought process, depending upon what information and opinions we are being exposed to. Unavoidably, this bias develops exponentially in line with the aggregate ideological leaning of your news feed (and it *will* always have a bias one way or the other). Social media is even structured to nurture this bias in quite an organic way; you will naturally want to build an environment that you enjoy being in, and social media will want to make that environment as easy to build as possible. It isn't necessarily a good or a bad thing, but it is often an unconscious process. The way we consume information now, and particularly the way young people consume information, means that all these subliminal developments regularly go not just unchallenged, but completely unnoticed. This subliminality, however, goes wider than news outlets and actual news stories; the people you have on your social media feed- your friends and family- and precisely what *they* share, are perhaps the main factor in your online environment and as such, the main tributaries to the problem. Why? Echo chambers.

I have alluded to these mythical echo chambers of ignorance a few times in this account, though not by this explicit name, and have as yet omitted any definition or classification. When referring to an echo chamber, one alludes to the relative silence of an opinion until it is bounced around a personal, trusted and similarly interested group of people, and so often on the internet-sphere liked, shared and repeated- echoed- into wrongly assumed factuality, granted an auspicious credence, where eventually little more than loud, distorted versions of the mother opinion are audible, and any counter argument is drowned out and ultimately, ignored.

In them, one is rendered ignorant to one's own opinion because of a *reluctance* or *inability* to observe oneself as "wrong". They are the assertion that the flute sounds divine, regardless of the flautist. The collective result of these chambers, these insulated vehicles of opinion, is the perpetuation of ignorance, of bigotry (cleverly associated with the right but equally if not more so practiced by the left), and of animosity. Echo chambers by their very nature harbour and incubate bias. But it tends not to be seen this way; more often than not, these fortresses of misconception are seen as sanctuaries of identity, places to establish your intellectual self, and reinforce opinions without much conflict until they are so engrained that they are battle ready. Echo chambers are for this reason so often passively sought out, and the environments within them given much more intellectual weight than they ought to be.

Opinions within them are divided more into categories of "right and wrong" than of right and left; generally speaking, little time is given to explaining the politics or philosophy behind a statement within an echo chamber, because amongst other things, there is simply *no need.* The very idea of there being places where there is *no need* for critical thinking should be a point of alarming realisation for anyone concerned with pursuing truth. People within echo chambers *accept* the arguments presented or witnessed because they *want* to, because they are popular within their respective chamber (by definition) and because they are common ground upon which to build relationships. Disagreement is naturally abrasive. Should we be in the echo chamber of popular culture revering Russell Brand as a political maverick, for example, we might be inclined to accept the opinions we come across because, in a flurry of articulation and charisma, his political ineptitude and irrelevance is painted in such a way as to engage core demographics, as to engage people who already agreeably think what he is saying, and encourage them to feel like they *know* that what he is saying is exactly how things are, *precisely true.*

In political echo chambers, people are often *soliciting their own ignorance* based on loose preconceptions and opinions being reinforced by someone who's only academic authority on the subject of politics and ideology is their number of followers, the amount of noise they can generate; how many people *echo* their sentiment. To be sure, there is a line of thought centred around the idea that all politics is predicated on this idea to some degree, but celebrity and personality politics take it to the nth degree. Remember, coming back to Russell Brand, he is the man that in 2013 told his loyal following that there is no point voting because "they're all the same"[6], and presumably after some pay-out, or some deal, told the same loyal following in 2015 that he was voting for Ed Miliband and Labour[7]. An "egalitarian Marxist"[8] telling people to vote for an at the time free market supporting, austerity practising, left-of-centre Labour party still plagued with the warmongering Blairites whom he so despises. Or at least despised... Either way, ignorant to this fact by choice, his

---

[6] Russell Brand telling people not to vote <https://www.bbc.co.uk/news/av/uk-24648651/russell-brand-i-ve-never-voted-never-will>

[7] Russel Brand tells people to vote Labour < https://www.theguardian.com/politics/2015/may/04/russell-brand-changes-mind-about-voting-and-urges-support-for-labour>

[8] Russel Brand ideological self-identification <https://www.businessinsider.com/russell-brand-explains-his-political-views-2014-12?r=UK>

following (largely students and young people), entrapped in the captivating aura of the media and its undeniable influence, hailed him as a messiah of political theory, a real step towards positive change.

This is another pernicious proclivity of echo chambers: that they produce hypocrites. I often wonder to myself why things like hypocrisy are seen as "negative" qualities. Preaching something but actually practising the opposite ought not to be an intrinsically bad thing; that is the nature of philosophy- fluid, adaptable, changing and subjective. However, in politics specifically, such incongruences as illustrated in the previous paragraphs exemplify some of the issues with hypocrisy; most pressingly, that it accommodates and facilitates ignorance.

If someone in politics is allowed to be hypocritical, they are allowed to be nakedly *deceitful*. If they are allowed to be hypocritical, they are allowed to be sneaky, allowed to be conceited, allowed to be fundamentally misinformed, and they are given a free pass to practice these negative intellectual qualities. Hypocrisy by definition requires deception in its execution; there *has* to be an element of skulduggery. It also, thusly, illustrates a lacking ability to make sound judgement on the behalf of the hypocrite, as an individual. Why should we trust a hypocrite? Why is what is better for us not better for *them*? Michael Gove shattered his reputation when, after incrementally tightening legislation around cocaine possession for public sector workers, he admitted to taking the drug himself, on numerous occasions[9]. Considering some of the ideas Gove was toying with involved lifetime bans for teachers caught with any class A drug, and in the same consideration remembering that Gove claimed to be reformed after his previous illicit drug use was brought to light, this whole scenario produces some questions. For example, is reform impossible? If not, why would a lifetime ban make any sense? If so, why in God's name is Gove still holding public office? Why oh why indeed... But at least he gives us a window into the ambiguity that is caused by hypocrisy.

The damage to the hypocrite does not stop there. The opponent, when arguing or debating *against* a hypocrite, is in a position to choose exactly what he wants to believe; he is given options. He can choose, when confronting a hypocrite, which side of their argument he wants to accept as true; not only that, but he can change sides should their opponent's riposte to his criticism suffice his tests of integrity. They- the hypocrite- are essentially fighting a war

---

9 Gove on his cocaine use: <https://www.politicshome.com/news/uk/political-parties/conservative-party/news/104442/michael-gove-denies-being-hypocrite-over>

on two fronts. Hypocrisy is careless, and carelessness is the mother of fragile argument. The negativity of hypocrisy is intrinsic in its reality; in the fact that to be a hypocrite you render yourself and your position ideologically vulnerable to attack and expose your own intellectual weaknesses and incongruences. Echo chambers encourage this hypocrisy, this intellectual dishonesty, in how they limit and close the boundaries of discussion. In a world of information saturation, hypocrisy when coupled with ignorance is dangerous, and echo chambers are houses of danger.

The Subliminal.

Throughout our early years, our young impressionable minds are saturated with a patchwork of information which only gets more convoluted as we move into adolescence and beyond. With information saturation- which is to say, the exposure to more information that any mind can reasonably expect to take in- there will always invariably be a lot of things quickly forgotten and there will also be plenty of information missed altogether. Some of the information we are exposed to, however, is never meant to be registered, and this is one of the more odious elements of how the majority of our political development is influenced in the modern day. There is a persistent subliminality with which our intellectual development is affected throughout regular and daily life. Throughout two of the most important avenues of this development, education and the media to which we are constantly and increasingly exposed, the practice (both consciously and unconsciously) of delivering information in an intentionally ambiguous way is as widespread as it is contemptible. We are force fed information subliminally, whether we acknowledge it or not, and we have a reflexive tendency to subliminally react.

This subliminality is produced by our direct environments, and in recent years has become increasingly influenced most specifically and potently by our direct *online* environment and the political eco system within. With this concept in mind, and considering that the very idea of social media is to follow, interact and keep in touch with your friends, we must simultaneously consider another curious idea which has been highlighted and stress tested by social media: the idea that it is always more favourable to agree with your friends than to disagree, particularly when it comes to politics and philosophy. This is because political animosity - which is ultimately in essence disagreement on how humanity should seek to properly exist, how humanity ought to be- is much more damaging and testing on one's tolerances and convictions than for example musical or literary disagreement. Indeed, often this is the case, and we find ourselves surrounded with politically like minds because of how naturally insufferable we find those with extensively different politics to our own, which in an attempt to avoid conflict and friction, sees us settle into our comfortable and *most acceptable* ideological habitat.

Not only are our perceptions of ideology and philosophy (separate from, but often synonymous with our morality) largely engineered by our direct environments, but they are also often developed and refined by them. Coupled with this, we also have an obvious and reasonable susceptibility to the doctrine of authority figures in our lives, from our parents, family and teachers, to our friends and work peers, many of whom tend populate our social media feeds. We often don't actively consider this at all in our daily actions, but the typography of our media environments shapes a subliminal perception of what are the absolutely *academic* disciplines of philosophy; not least because the audience you have is likely to affect the content you deem relevant, relative or acceptable for them to see. To illustrate this, have you ever had a thought that you would like to have posted on social media but censored yourself because you didn't want your mum or boss to see it? The act of this unconscious omission, over any substantial period of time, directly affects how you are likely to think about things and to a more nuanced degree, how you are likely to perceive. This consideration is not new- how you act down the pub is analogous to it- but the broad and profound extent to which it applies on social media is completely new to the modern age.

It is with this passive self-censorship and the proliferation of echo chambers that much of our philosophical and political understanding -at least in the early years of our development, but often well beyond- is now shaped in the post social media world. Legitimate as this narrow experience is to the forging of political opinion and personal *wants*, it is not very conducive in producing actual *understanding* of those wants; knowledge is not the power, understanding is. If people know what they want from politics but not how it is achieved politically, then, forgetting their own limitations, they render themselves vulnerable to the repetitive, cyclical politics of things like the gift manifesto; the phenomenon we see of shiny parcels of policy wrapped in overtly suggestive ideological packaging- £10 an hour minimum wage wrapped in "for the many not the few"- and we are always, inevitably, angry when it doesn't *quite* happen the way that those shiny parcels were sold; ignorance breeds anger.

What it also does is allow for politicians to hold a unique grasp of ideological authority provided they suppose to answer the often-difficult questions generated by life, and they are afforded a lax adherence to ideology by the general populations' lacking understanding thereof. We see this concept best exemplified by the workings of the Alistair Campbell's of the world; of political spin doctors in the form of political spin, precisely because people have a necessarily limited exposure to critical thinking in their political and philosophical development.

Political spin is king, and it affords politicians and political institutions vast swathes of power. They seize the social opportunities presented by the general ignorance of the population to the deep and complex concepts of ideology and philosophy which shape and impact *everything* about our daily lives. The widely cited public sentiment that "they're all the same" holds water in that politicians *do* all practice this appropriation of emotion and ignorance in its broadest sense, and attempt to capitalise upon them. Our broad and deep ignorance of the very fundamentals of ideology, philosophy and politics is the currency they convert into votes, into political capital: into power.

Subliminality is how almost all of our political understanding is primarily shaped in early life; even in later life, to a large extent. Because we don't specifically look to study politics, philosophy or ideology in anywhere near the detail with which we study other hyper complex disciplines, the development of our perceptions is left to the symbiosis of opinion through the implicit and subliminal lessons happening throughout all avenues of our lives, all aspects of interaction and every instance of cooperation. This is a bad thing in so far as all of our collective political development, aside from that of an acute minority, is infected by interpretation and expression of political positions and concepts by those who again, in general, have had little to no formal study of these three major concepts throughout their lives and are nevertheless in a position to deliver their doctrine; sometimes, as in the case of teachers and educators, even to a captive and profoundly malleable audience.

This construction of philosophical, ideological and political perception on a foundation of intellectual sand then proliferates across generations. We see the study of politics and philosophy in any serious capacity relegated to the time and minds of comparatively few within society, and yet they are probably the disciplines which have fundamentally had the most impact throughout history, and are the disciplines likely to have the most impact going forward. The net result of all of this- the passive introduction we have to the concepts of politics, ideology and philosophy in early life, the borderline indoctrination of young minds at the hands of the implicitly biased authority figures in their lives, and the usurping of that influential position by the media, fuelled by the dishonest pursuit of an opaque agenda, is that we have created a positive feedback loop of ignorance in society. We have created a monster.

III
The Power of Ignorance.

"The effect of liberty to individuals is, that they may do what they please. We ought to see what it will please them to do, before we risque congratulations"- Edmund Burke.

In this marvellously modern era of Google, Internet connectivity, social media, networking on a truly global scale and unprecedented progress with Science and education, people don't often seriously entertain the idea of universal ignorance. The idea of universal ignorance is the idea that not only are most people ignorant to most things[10], but that the problem is getting worse, not better. As information becomes increasingly available it seems that we become increasingly averse to critical thinking in tandem with it. The lack of this critical thinking is the contributing factor to this ignorance; a good analogy of this principle is revealed when we stop to consider how exposed we are in our

---

10 Sloman, S. and Fernbach, P., n.d. *The Knowledge Illusion.* This is a difficult matter of fact to argue because of the implication (and in no small part the brashness of the necessary language used), but it is absolutely and universally true that no matter who you are, the things that you *do not* know or understand will always, without exception, vastly outnumber the things that you *do* know and understand.

daily routines to words and language, but how desperately reliant we are becoming on predictive text and spell check.

However, because of this increasing and intensifying exposure to information, most people, with a little push from a media source they trust, can today be convinced to simultaneously believe that they are intellectually superior to the majority, and as such that their opinion as such always matters; a luxury afforded by this perceived superiority. It isn't so hard to identify this principle in action either; have you ever seen someone online tell an opponent to "read a book"? What "book" specifically, and more importantly- why? Most people present their opinions as arguments, and are looking for reasons to be correct more than they will look for reasons to change their mind, evidence that they might be wrong or that their truth might not be so absolute. A simple observation at face value, but an extraordinarily profound observation when one considers the implications it has for ignorance, intellect, free thinking and the health of the mind.

People so often confuse this idea- that they are well educated, ideologically savvy political thinkers- with the reality that is them being extremely well versed on their own refined *moral* and political positions; this is the phenomenon of people en-masse not realising that their perceptions of ideological 'right and wrong' (including moral perceptions of policy) are always testaments of *personal* morality, and passive ones at that. In the spirit of this, political observations and judgments are *always* subjective, and correct or right to the arguer (true), but- and this is crucial- they are so often argued on the assumptive premise of them being *objective* and universally applicable; always right and correct to *everyone* (factual).

Meaning Is Not Fixed.

These arguments are generally presented in such a way as to both purposefully and accidentally avoid proper philosophical scrutiny and evade the intricacies of ideology. How can you intend to accidentally avoid scrutiny? You present a position that is *likely* to steer the discussion a certain way, skilfully or otherwise, and as such avert any critical gaze from that which might not be coherent to that which you want in focus. Presenting, for example, an argument around minority oppression is not likely to develop into a discussion of *whether* minorities are oppressed, but more the *extent* to their oppression. This limited scope for exploring ideas is often not intentional but regularly becomes the case, if not the norm. People can be told that something is *right,* as over simplistic as that word itself makes any implication or concept it refers to, without ever having any education on the two subjects of philosophy or ideology, and as such no understanding of the flexibility or the metaethical and epistemological difficulties[11] in describing something as 'moral', 'right' or 'correct'. Fundamentally, what is meant by *right*, and what is it to be *correct*? And how do they *specifically* differ between situations?

These questions may sound straight forward or simple but are of extreme and paramount importance to one's political (and wider) understanding. More than that, these questions are fundamental to explaining how we as a species understand anything. For example, many were opposed to the bedroom tax in the UK on the moral grounds that it bullied and targeted the poor (seemingly but perhaps not always an unquestionable evil), where in all reality it was an ideologically classical liberal mechanism towards minimising government expenditure, whilst imploring private ownership of property[12]. The fact it affected social housing was indiscriminate of tenants' financial status, social status or class allegiance, and the fact that most affected people were low or zero earners was a by-product, the aftermath - as the classical liberal will undoubtedly assure you- of increased state intervention, pseudo socialist and "big tent" policy overseen by Brown and Blair's third-way New Labour, resulting in an entrenched over reliance of the population on the state and by proxy, wider society.

The so called "bedroom tax" was as ideologically motivated as it was politically motivated; arguably more so. It was not a lateral or superfluous opportunity for the Tory party to 'punish the poor', or any other easy, predictable, pseudo political observation; it was the produce of the party following the direction of an ideology, and the ideology that motivated it should therefore have been the subject of people's critique, should they be the paragons of intellect and knowledge which they would have us believe them to be (and often believe themselves to be). However, they are not, and consequently these surface level criticisms came flooding in, these assertions of 'right-wing extremism' (whatever that even means nowadays) reared their media fuelled heads, and the virtuous status of this valiant resistance was ironclad in nothing but peoples' ignorance. And yes, this happens on the right as well. People cannot ask for intelligent debate and bring with them to the table a

---

[11] That is to say, the difficulties in establishing actual meaning in context and true understanding of intent, application and situational usefulness

[12] Exemplified by the British classically liberal tradition, as defined by Friedrich Hayek, amongst others.

portfolio filled with ill-informed anecdotes of 'right' and 'wrong' and hollow, weightless morality, whilst also remaining ignorant to even the most basic foundations of their assertions and arguments.

And yet, people do regularly practice this exact kind of misinformation. We see articles of 'hard right Brexit strategy'[13] and 'bad deals for Scotland'[14], oceans of misinformation about education, transport and health; we see ideological critique presented circumstantially, so as to imply and assert it as fact, and as such people develop false political narratives to vent their anger. Similar to blaming the apple for falling on your head, and thus, in laying the blame squarely on the apple, allowing gravity and the tree to enjoy a life free of criticism for their role in your plight. It is as imperative to politics that people understand that ideas align with ideology, which is born of philosophy, as it is for people to know that it is gravity pulling the apple from a sufficiently weakened tree. Yet as the culpability of gravity and biology is often overlooked in such a scenario, so too is the culpability of philosophy overlooked in the ideological development and implementation of policy.

Capturing emotion.

This point draws one's attention towards the precise kind of accessible ignorance that *could* be inspiring the often negative emotions towards media saturated politics that people now have. And these negative thoughts of the majority of people's emotional involvement with politics, ideology and philosophy is an interesting thing, indicative of ignorance to the disciplines. This isn't a suggestion to run away from, as we so often do when the potential for us to be revealed as ignorant, stupid or uneducated is exposed and highlighted. This is a suggestion to *embrace.* Why is it that we are so often afraid of our intellectual flaws? And why is this fear particularly pronounced within the disciplines of politics and philosophy? Why is it that we are often so often hostile to their exposure? Why is it ignorance of these things *specifically* which agitates and infuriates people, especially when highlighted by an outsider, more so than their ignorance to things like thermonuclear physics, being able to speak another language or being able to code in C++?

---

13   <https://www.theguardian.com/commentisfree/2018/jun/13/brexit-traitor-trope-hard-right-fantasies-risk>

14 <https://www.bbc.co.uk/news/uk-scotland-scotland-politics-46207184>

These implications also suggest, by proxy, that most people have not an academic relationship with politics, philosophy or ideology, but more of an emotive one; that politics is often understood by the emotions we experience when discussing the political. For this reason, in a *de facto* sense we do all have an automatic legitimacy when we discuss politics outside of the academic spheres, but we have to be cautious with how we exercise this authority; the distinction between the anecdotal and the academic is often lost with this discussion, and it is an important distinction to maintain

Philosophy, ideology and politics are present in our daily lives at every possible juncture of existence, across every tier of relationship, between every individual interaction. In acknowledging this, we ought to also acknowledge that there should be some separation of politics, ideology and philosophy into two individually understood but parallel tiers: the anecdotal and the academic. The music you make with friends is different to the music we hear in opera houses or on film soundtracks, and usually for good reason. Within the anecdotal, in politics as music, every individual's opinion and input is equally valid, as subjective experience is king and, by definition, unique to us all. Within the academic spheres of discussion, however, a more scientific approach is needed, and an educated understanding of politics, ideology and philosophy is demanded. Anecdotal discussion seeks to offer opinion, academic discussion ought to seek truth. Unfortunately, the terms of separation between these spheres is difficult to not only define, but also enforce in any meaningful way.

This is because these disciplines are responsible, to varying but always prevalent degrees, for every political decision, every legislative proposal and every legal dispute; for everything. These disciplines have an eclectic effect on everyone's lives, and as such it stands to reason that everyone ought to have the ability to scrutinise, challenge, support and oppose them. It also stands to reason, however, that most people are not going to intentionally discuss things like reduction of taxes through the intellectual lens of John Stuart Mill's utilitarianism, Edmund Burke's conservatism, John Locke's classical liberalism or Karl Marx's Marxism. People are going to discuss them based on how changes in spending make them *feel*, or their subjective and unique reactions to the impact of whichever changes they are commenting on. They will offer emotional responses; the anecdotal over the academic, often encouraged by their aforementioned bubble of influence. Coupled with this, politics as a discipline falls victim to the tendency we all have of most passionately responding to that which we receive negatively, and because of this many of those responses are predictably and regularly manifest themselves in two things: anger and fear.

Both of these emotions are easily weaponised by anyone seeking control over another, or seeking to acquire any position of power. Media bosses and the social media top brass spring to mind here, as for them power is money (which implies that fear and anger are money, a very sinister implication indeed), but most importantly for us this rule applies most saliently to the political classes. If they can usurp your emotion, they can conquer your mind and in doing so, secure your support. Hence, when an agenda needs pushing or elections come around, the two gold standard emotions to tap into are usually anger and fear. Whether the source of that anger or fear be the paycheques of the 1%, as it so often is for the left, or eastern European migration for the right, it can be weaponised by an appropriately Machiavellian mind and processed into capital.

Political concepts are so often reduced to an emotional soundbite or buzzword, and the fear they inspire is a construct, on the whole, of agendas. Fear and anger both have a natural penchant for being able to trigger a response and manufacture a conversation. This fear can be accredited to people's lack of ideological understanding, and it serves a great many purposes[15]. All interactions are political. When you walk into any business, the business owner will likely be nice, courteous and accommodating to you. Why is this? Is the business owner just a lovely, upstanding citizen? Or are they simply creating an environment in which you're willing to spend your money? Are business owners nicer to you when you have more money than if you have less, or none? The same logic here can be applied with great utility to politicians, and it regularly is. If there is a single class of person of which we as citizens are universally sceptical, it is them, precisely for this reason. Everything they say or do seems to be for personal gain; their agenda is always hiding in plain sight. The point is that everyone has an agenda, and those agendas usually require the manipulation of a situation. That manipulation, whether it be a shopkeeper's genuine agenda to make small talk and skilfully choose what he thinks you *might* want to hear, or some publication's intentional spin at the behest of that particular publication's editor, is tailored to the respective situations they appropriate. They can do this because people may well know of these agendas, but seldom do they *understand* them. Politicians rely on the ambiguous nature to capture and profiteer from emotions, and the most valuable of them all is fear.

---

[15] This is expressed supremely well in: Peterson, J.B. (1999). *Maps of meaning: the architecture of belief.* New York; London: Routledge. The interpretation of fear found in this book could be said as being centred around Peterson's explanations, and the understandings generated therein, although with some caveats.

If we work with the presumption, for the moment, that a phobia is "an irrational fear", then we can partly attribute that irrationality to a lack of understanding. An arachnophobe fears the spider because of little more than a lack of understanding. Some entertainers hold and handle even black widow spiders, despite their refined and astute knowledge that these spiders are dangerous, because they *understand* them. This understanding doesn't make the spider, of itself, intrinsically any less dangerous, but it does mean that the understander is equipped to deal with the situation at hand. As such, whether the handler receives a bite or dances with death unscathed, his *understanding* of the mortal peril with which he is faced- not just his knowledge- is an elite enlightenment that facilitates his survivability.

Compare this to the arachnophobes *perceived* and skewed interpretation of danger. The arachnophobe enters the situation in a sense of panic, a heightened and exaggerated emotional state, because of limiting perceptions that the savvy handler doesn't fall victim to. They are much more likely to arrive at ignorance afforded conclusions, and to make ignorance afforded mistakes, even though they know of the danger with which they are faced.

The handlers understanding negates fear, in its simplest context[16], and defuses within them the angry, knee jerk response to the unknown that so often manifests itself in emotions like animosity, aggression and even hatred; at the most basic level, negativity. Truly understanding the enemy, whether that be an arachnid or an ideology, equips one with the tools to handle and challenge it. There is an old adage that goes something like 'knowledge is power'; I would contest this. I would argue that actually, it is *understanding* that gives us power. Knowledge without understanding is an empty glass; you have the right vessel to carry some nutritious morning orange juice, and as such the glass has the *potential* to satisfy and energize you for the morning because of its capacity to hold a drink. But without the orange juice, that potential is squandered, and your thirst will persist. Knowledge is the vessel with which one can achieve understanding; but without understanding, like the empty glass without the juice, knowledge has no nutritional value, no use of itself. Without understanding, it has no intellectual nor practical merit.

As a final illustration of my point here, to hopefully substantiate my ramblings, I have an equation: $E = mc^2$. Almost everyone reading this will *know* of the equation; that is to say, they know of it. But I put it to you that very few

---

16 *Ibid.*

people, without using the Achilles tendon of intellect that is google, actually *understand* it. To assert my surety one step further, I would suggest that even upon a rapid google search, and the newly acquired (but perhaps quickly forgotten) knowledge that E= energy, m= mass, c^2 = the speed of light squared and the equation goes some way to explaining how very minuscule quantities of mass such as atoms can release huge amounts of energy, the majority of people outside the world of physics still don't truly *understand* it. At least, I still lack this understanding, regardless of the fact that I know of the equation and its implementation. Knowledge is useless without an understanding of consequence, implementation or utility.

A Matter of Interpretation.

Interestingly, people *will* allow themselves to be incorrect when it comes to lots of areas of academia, and even life. Often, they will accept their ignorance to subjects such as astrophysics, mathematics, engineering or even painting, and will accept that they really have only two options: either readily concede that they have no business practising astrophysics and essentially remove astrophysics from their world, or endeavour to educate themselves into astrophysical relevance. The same can be said for mathematics. Mathematics is almost the intellectual parody, the classic "marmite" subject where people will readily tell you if they have little or no understanding of more so than perhaps any other subject, and will also openly assure you of their disinterest in acquiring any new understanding of the subject. Fair enough; we do after all only require the bare minimum mathematical understanding on a day to day basis.

However, these readily observable admissions arouse the question: why is critique of ideological and political understanding met with such animosity and conflict? Particularly visible online, people left, right and centre use this critique as a weapon and try to assure their ideological adversaries of *their* stupidity, *their* ignorance, *their* bigotry or *their* absolute lack of understanding. All too often this boils down to a discourse of insult throwing, soundbite repetition and pointless 'google facts'. The narrative surrounding ideology and politics, unique to the subjects, is one of perpetual aggression, disagreement, antagonism, pseudo intellectuality and desperation to claim one's mastery of the subject. Why is this the case?

Perhaps the answer here lies in two things: again, the inextricably sentient emotional reflex that is fear, and context. Fear, inspired by the intense way we perceive the ideology or doctrine against which we are positioned, and the context of how we perceive our counter position. Essentially, how you see and perceive your 'enemies' and how you understand your own ideological or political cause. This is crucially important: mathematics, astrophysics, engineering and painting, to a certain extent, are socially renowned "do or do not's". It is acceptable to admit to anyone and everyone that you either have the capacity to be one of these things or you don't. Not only that, but your such capacity can be uniformly *measured.*

The problem with philosophy, ideology and as such politics is that they are almost entirely *subjective*; there is essentially no such thing as a 'wrong' opinion. Fear is thusly inspired not explicitly in the policy, or the end product of ideological thought, but *implicitly* in the volatility and scope of our perceptions of ideology (both the perceptions of the thinker, the interpretation of whom being paramount to the likely outcome of adopting an ideology, and the perceptions of critic, the perceptions of whom dictate their specific interpretations of how the ideology in question will materialise). Fear is inspired by the conclusions you have drawn as to what *might* or *could* happen; the *potential* as opposed to precisely what *will* happen, or the reality (because that is naturally impossible to predict). Ergo, the Tory (the thinker) is not dangerous until the communist (the critic) individually perceives Tory (as in, Conservative party) philosophy, and as such concludes the development of Tory ideology as "dangerous".

In ideology, we can only do this because of a fundamental and contextual misunderstanding of the principalities of danger: attributing a characteristic to an ideology, or to stick with the example at hand, attributing 'danger' to 'Tory' henceforth synonymises all things Tory, all things linked to that position, as dangerous. Just that quickly, this attribution cements the narrative of 'danger' in the mind and thoughts of the critic as a response to any 'Tory" stimulus.

To call an ideology dangerous is to imply that it stands to cause harm to someone or something. The "someone or something" in the case of ideology is another ideology, its disciples, and their agenda. As such we should realise that ideology can *only* be dangerous to other ideologies, and also only in principle, because, by their very nature, ideologies are born of the desire to improve or benefit, in one way or another, a group of peoples' lives, or- more precisely- their existence. This must (and does) mean, therefore, that one ideology's methods of achieving this will directly, often and naturally conflict with those of others. Any threat to one ideology's such methods by another's is an intrinsic danger to that ideology. If I, for example, want to achieve "fairness", I will first have to have an idea of what specifically "fairness" means to *me*, and then I will have to build a political roadmap to implement it. If your idea of "fairness" is incompatible with mine, then the political roadmap I build might inspire *fear,* because of its perceived *danger* to your interpretation of fairness and your suggested political route to achieving it. That isn't to say that *my* interpretation is objectively dangerous; just that it is dangerous to *you.*

Make no mistake, this is not to suggest that it is *wrong* to deduce ideology as dangerous; *all* ideologies have the capacity to be deduced as dangerous. But I am suggesting that should you make such a deduction, there ought to be two caveats to it. Firstly, that it should be a conscious decision to do so based on an *academic, learned* understanding of philosophy, ideology and politics[17], not some perceived understanding of one's own opinion, akin to how drawing the blueprints for a building should be based on an *academic* knowledge of construction, not one's uneducated opinion as to how a building ought to look; we all have the capacity to draw a building and even envision what a cool, useful or "good" building looks like, but we are *not* all qualified architects. Secondly, that it should be actively realised that this perceived danger is directly and inextricably relevant to the thinker- to you, specifically (and perhaps those like-minded)- but it is *never universally applicable.* Interpretation is key, and it is within this interpretation that we see both good and bad presumptions of ideology materialise.

The Nazi and the Liberal.

Allow me the chance to present an example, because I appreciate the convoluted and heavy style of my writing and feel this point requires further substantiation: There is no danger (and ergo nothing to be *feared*) by Nazi ideology to the Nazi: amongst their ideology, they see a social problem- a 'lower' or 'unpure' race or group of people, such as Jews, Blacks, Gypsies, minorities etc- and they see a *perceived as reasonable* solution in concentration camps, murder and genocide. Sure, there is immediate danger to minorities, but to make a point of that is somewhat null, a straw man, as implicitly in the development of Nazism[18] it is stipulated that genetics and ethnicity are pivotal to ones standing, relevance and prominence in society.

---

17 Of which *very* few individuals *truly* have, a point which ought to be received as though it is meant in as well intending and *de facto* sense as it is possible to mean.

18 Specifically the Nazism of 1930s Germany, the Nazism we all understand as being implied when discussed, although I am aware as to the intellectual flexibility to the ideology.

Similarly, there is no danger in communism to the communist; they, like the Nazi, see a problem- often in their case the idea of land ownership, private ownership in general, in the class system, in the unequal distribution of wealth and indeed, the very idea of private wealth and crystallised capital, and see no problem in the mass murder of private landowners, the aristocracy, bankers and anyone deemed a threat to the communist agenda (and often, as it worked out, the inevitable communist state). To suggest that communism is 'dangerous'- and as such something to be feared- to a member of the bourgeoisie or a free marketeer is a moot point; communism disagrees with and seeks to eradicate class and wealth disparity. It is intrinsically, expectedly and fairly hostile to those t sees as enemies.

However, both these ideologies inspire some degree of fear in the Liberal, classical or neo (but not so much postmodern), and the values and *perceived* ideological doctrine that they, as a liberal thinker, would champion. This is an interesting point insofar as Liberalism is an ideology in its own right, and now offers a conclusive perspective of comparison: the Liberal fears the communist or Nazi regime just as much as the communist fears bourgeoisie control, or Nazism fears the death of the master race or the 'weakness' of Liberal politics. Suddenly, as opposed to viewing Nazism or Communism as doctrines of hatred, we can observe them as doctrines of fear: their entire conception is through fear and distain for a different school of thought or cause, such that it unites people in the same conclusions. One has just as much urisdiction to assert Nazism or Communism as 'wrong' as both of those deologies have to assert the irrelevance and corruption- the wrongness- of iberalism, particularly neo-Liberal western democracy, which is a direct deological threat (with its coveting of capital, free market fetish and doctrine of tolerance) to the likes of Nazism and communism.

Liberal democracy *is* a danger to communism, as far as the communist is concerned, in so much as it's philosophy and the politics it bears *directly* oppose and constrict the doctrine of communism. As such, we arrive at the apex of what this small chapter has been seeking to convey: neither the Nazi, the communist nor the classical or neoliberal is empirically *wrong or dangerous*. It would be academically misguided and irresponsible to assert otherwise, as all strands of thought are manifest in the sanctuary of opinion, and are as such afforded the luxury of evading (at least in an ideological capacity) the damning conclusion of objectively 'right' or 'wrong'. Indeed, that assessment is the reserve of the ongoing metaethical, ontological and epistemological debates, and is unlikely to conclude any time soon. No ideology is *wrong* until you, as a earned thinker and individual understand and reveal the incompatibilities of the reality of its politics and its foundational philosophy: by definition, you cannot have Liberal communism just as much as you cannot have communist Liberalism (although, some may argue this as *de facto* socialism[19]), because the philosophies of both ideologies are so disparate and the policy and end goals that both seek to generate are so different.

Intellectual Pluralism

Conclusively, two things should be observed here: firstly, that not only is fear subjective[20], but also that it is an incredibly versatile agent of control. To make an individual *hate* another, or more relevantly, to make a person hate an ideology, one simply has to make them *scared* of it; to echo the sentiment of Machiavelli, it is much easier to be feared than to be loved, and much easier to inspire fear than to inspire love[21]. Secondly, the power of ideology and its capacity to capture fear lies in its intrinsic subjectivity, which has an inherit elasticity of definition due to the average layperson's lack of actual ideological understanding; and make no mistake, the concept of ideology is far from understood, let alone a subject of academic consensus.

Illustratively, there is no *per se* Tory ideology; it is a (supposedly) right-of-centre doctrine focused broadly around classical and neoliberal principalities, as well as the broad philosophy of conservatism. Three main strands of Conservative, or Tory, ideology have dominated since 1834- one nationism, Burkean conservatism and neo-liberal Thatcherism- varying in ideological direction by as much as embracing border-line collectivism, to absolute state reductionism. It is a *party* founded on ideological principles, a pluralist vessel of ideological implementation, *not* an ideology in its own right. If you are scared of 'austerity', for example, and join a party based on its "anti-Tory austerity" stance, you aren't throwing your support behind an ideology but a melting pot

---

19 Because specifically of the fact that employing liberal ideology in the pursuit of communist goals would potentially create an atmosphere one could describe as "democratic socialist". I do not, however, agree with this and am merely outlining the potential interpretation, if for nothing else to exemplify the overlying point that ideology is fluid.

20 In so far as what should and should not be feared is in the eye of the beholder, as is the degree to which they ought to be feared

21 Niccolò Machiavelli and Goodwin, R. (2003). *The prince*. Boston: Dante University Press, chapter XVII *"Concerning Cruelty And Clemency, And Whether It Is Better To Be Loved Than Feared"*

of *ideologies*. Parties are responsible for implementing ideological positions, not presenting ideologies. Manifestos are shopping lists of policy guided by ideologies, not a specific ideology (in the purest sense). The Tory stance on austerity is the result of the party implementing an ideological position, not *creating* one, and any parties counter position likewise.

The conflation of these principles leads to some suspect and sometimes sinister rhetoric when discussing policies. Austerity isn't the rich taking from the poor to the Tory, the Conservative party member and party loyalist. At its core, it is the idea of reducing government expenditure to reduce the influence of the government on the individual and with it, the size of the state. With the Thatcherite mantra readily to hand, the state cannot give to anyone without taking from someone. Obviously with this understanding, if the state disproportionately gives money to people that fall within the perceived bracket of "poor", then the state must take that money from someone else, usually (or so the argument often goes) from the "rich". Upon removing that state funding, the reverse will happen by default: the action of not taking money from the rich through taxation will disproportionately hit the "poor" in their pockets, and produce the argument that in not taking that money from the rich, they are essentially taking it from the poor. As such this idea of the Tories hating the poor because their policy favours and encourages individual accountability over those reliant on the state is firmly developed.

Perhaps based on this perspective it might be easier to understand or consider the ideology that produces Tory policy outside of narrow, faction based, adversarial interpretations; perhaps not. In either scenario, we are looking at the complex relationship between the institution of the political party and ideology in motion. We are looking at an illustration of the trepidation with which one should approach soundbite politics and ideological assimilation, as well as how easy it is to unintentionally avoid such trepidation altogether. What we are witnessing here is specifically how fear above all else manifests itself in political discourse, embeds itself in your chosen ideology and reveals itself in ideologies we don't understand.

Fear is essential to ideology. Fear is the leading currency with which ideology, in the modern social theatre, purchases power. It is an idea, to be captured and used to manipulate. Fear is the home of misinterpretation. Fear is the idea that truth is objective. Fear is the mistake of confusing knowledge as power. Fear is the easiest way to capture a mind. Fear is the basis of political opposition. Fear is not just useful; it's necessary, and it is so easily born of ignorance. It is something that the political party intentionally produces with a view to usurping power afforded by the support of the politically ignorant general lay population.

IV
The Media Influence.

"Who controls the past controls the future; who controls the present controls the past." - George Orwell

The rhetoric and politics we see on a daily basis are no accident. Newspapers and most news outlets have an explicit ideological agenda (even if that agenda is independence), and almost everything written on the internet is written through the lens of someone's opinion. Almost everything we see, from the banning of "beach body ready" adverts in London, to the soap operas that have begun featuring all black episodes[22], is a visualisation of an ideologically motivated answer to the questions of "can and should we show this?". We are constantly reading and watching the agenda of some editor or organization; someone's opinion. In fact, we always have been, since societies developed means of communication, from Socrates and his open-air preaching's, to the newspapers of the 1600s; for as long as man has been civilised, he has been adrift in a sea of opinionated, agenda driven media.

---

22 Such as the 2009 episode of EastEnders highlighted in this article <https://www.dailymail.co.uk/tvshowbiz/article-1153903/BBCs-black-episode-EastEnders-watched-8-4million-viewers.html>

Obviously, that media isn't necessarily all political (at least at face value), and over the centuries has developed and fed various narratives and causes quite successfully and for the betterment of humanity. I am not here to criticize the media, but to suggest that you, in the context of modernity, develop and forward these agendas almost entirely subliminally through things you freely ("freely") elect to watch, read and follow; follow being the concept we are most concerned with in the media world as it now is.

Look at your personal news feeds on social media platforms; do you follow plenty of arts pages? Plenty of media pages, such as IGN, Konbini, HuffPost? What about your friends? Do they share pages from specific sites more than others? Or, allow me to rephrase that: are there things your friends *would not* share, post, or openly follow? Are there people on twitter you follow just to insult, or people you follow just because of who *they* insult? All these considerations factor into the subconscious stream of information you are exposed to daily.

The Huffington post, for example, would never advertise an EDL rally, a BNP conference or even a Michael Caine film since he revealed his pro Brexit stance, and the action of *not* advertising the aforementioned is in fact a very conscious decision, a decision which will affect your outlook, as a follower. It might seem obvious- who in their right mind would advertise a BNP rally- but that obvious, almost axiomatic position we take *is* important. We are subjected to ideological and philosophical agendas constantly and rendered blind disciples to the messages they are trying to convey. Your Facebook newsfeed has a lot of power and influence over your thoughts and even your own ideological considerations. For example, if you are constantly seeing the Huff post running anti Tory, pro EU, pro Corbyn, anti-Putin, pro refugee stories, it stands to reason that not only will this be shaping your world view, but your perceptions of ideological doctrine and the broader political world.

This is something I think it's fair to suggest most people probably know of, but in the same vain they don't truly *understand*. Understanding, as we have addressed, is far superior to knowledge. People, through ignorance wilful or otherwise, seem to completely relegate the fact that their personal data is relentlessly harvested to produce an acutely personalised stream of information, which is then fed into the abyss of their unconscious and sorted into the category of "completely irrelevant". This is in many ways quite curious because we entered into the technological age with extreme trepidation and vigilance. Remember "Y2K" or the controversy when contactless payment was released? Where did that controversy go? In the wake of this short term memory and practiced indifference, people seem to simultaneously disregard the fact that not only is their data harvested by these social media platforms (and essentially sold back to them through targeted advertisements), but the data of the people and pages they follow is passively harvested, to an enormous and exceptionally acute degree- by *them*.

You are not just a supplier of information on an epic and completely unprecedented scale in the age of digital media; you are also a *harvester* of it. But you don't have an algorithm, data banks, organised folders or lines of adaptable code. Your senses are enigmatic and unpredictable. You cannot take and quantify data in the same way a machine does, and human memory works in strange, surreptitious and extraordinary ways; ways which render this data consumption by the individual largely as passive as the data provision.

A Broad Scope.

Whimsical ideas of Facebook manipulation momentarily aside, social media is a perfect contemporary example of the influence media has, as well as its *prospective* power. If you are not watching, explicitly, for political and ideological influence, then you will not find it, but that is not to say you won't be receptive to it. Is rape wrong? Of course it is. Is cold blooded murder wrong? Most people would probably suppose so. Is paedophilia wrong? Unequivocally, yes. These things are largely matters of public moral unity; that is to say, we don't need wider influencing as a society on these ideas (although they are regularly captured for the emotional revenue they can generate) because they are, to the western liberal general will[23], already set in stone.

But then, what about our attitudes towards, say, tax evasion? Is all taxation theft? Or is taxation the subscription we pay to live in a civilised society? Should earnings be capped at £1million? Or should we be free to amass an unlimited amount of wealth? Do Syrian migrants deserve sanctuary or are they well overstepping the mark in going through dozens of safe countries just to arrive specifically in Britain? These questions have much more real, contemporary political bite, and it is these questions and questions like them which are far from matters of public unity. This disagreement is what affords the media the power to capture our minds for revenue, both monetarily and politically, in terms of platform support. With the aforementioned societally agreed upon opinions (murder, rape, paedophilia), the drip feeding of

---

23 Rousseauian "general will" as outlined famously in The Social Contract: Rousseau, J. and Tozer, H. (1998). *The social contract*. Ware, UK: Wordsworth Editions Ltd.

information, manipulation and data isn't so much of a concern, because generally, people don't have any unanswered questions about these such moral axioms, and in general major political parties don't have any reason to challenge or alter them. They're *mostly* fine as they are. However, with the issues outlined at the beginning of this paragraph, there is an inherit scope and potential for our minds to be captured and our opinions to be swayed. There is as such a natural attraction to these undecided 'grey' issues because of the power they stand to afford anyone willing to mine them.

Coming back to the news feed influence, and recalling if we will the proclivity we have to react with anger or fear, if one is seeing things that one agrees with- either good or bad- one tends to pay little more notice than a passing affirmation of support, maybe a nod to oneself or a groan of self-assurance. However, often upon seeing something one disagrees with, a plethora of emotional responses and possible consequences become suitable prospective reactions to these opinions and the publication that gave them a platform. If our anger gets the better of us, in such a situation we may be tempted to offer our disapproval, and it is now easier than ever to register such disapproval in the age of social media and slacktivism. A myriad of actions are available to us, but for now the actions which most command our interrogative concern are the unfriend, unfollow or delete options.

These options allow for an individual to express their anguish quickly, efficiently, quantifiably and visibly. People can see when you dislike something; people can feel the loss of you following them; people feel the weight of being unfriended. We are often more inclined to express our dislike in a more pronounced and obvious way. We are often more inclined- particularly in an online environment- to argue against the things we dislike; it is no secret that the digital wall inspires within people a heightened sense of bravery and vigilance. We engage in debates, arguments and interactions more and more as a collective group, and particularly *where* we engage in these actions is important, because usually engagement translates into profit. Social media platforms what these engagements there, and different media outlets want these engagements on their page. Individuals want confirmation from within these pages by other individuals engaging in online warfare. These 'grey' issues encourage interaction, abet platform growth and afford those able to acquire your digital capital increasingly powerful.

Publications and media pages looking to grow are, therefore, incentivised to generate, chase and weaponise these interactions, and above all else avoid being unfollowed or unfriended; being "disliked" is fair enough, because it is, at least, engagement. Precisely because publications are incentivised in this way is the epicentre of concern here; namely, that they are not incentivised to do it in any amicable or productive way. They play on the very human desire to be heard, and the western desire to be morally virtuous. They want to be involved as much online as they possibly can, they want to be shared into relevance or infamy and they want to go viral. The want for those outcomes specifically is what brings a perverse danger along with it. For when we combine the fact that publications chase interactions, and the idea that negativity has a proclivity to generate more interaction, we arrive at a formula for profit reliant on both engagement and hostility. As well as this, they are incentivised to hyperbolise whatever they can to generate these interactions, and through this hyperbole we see narratives develop and change; even the extent to which narratives are pronounced has changed in the age of social media, with hostility perhaps more vicious and partisan than we have ever seen before.

Crucially, what this has meant for the average person and the societies they are a part of is that when we see things we disagree with nowadays, we tend to attack the publication or person giving that opinion, because this is precisely what we are encouraged to do. We fail to constructively critique or explore the opinion itself because there is no immediate motivator to do so, or immediate reward from offering such thought, and we often see no intellectual problem in doing so. Rarely do people fundamentally dismantle and truly, honestly, *think*, in the philosophical context, about *'what'*, *'how'* and *'why'* anymore. We generally pay no attention to the fundamentals of what exactly it is we are attacking or challenging and continue doing so in the bliss of our own ignorance, in a world increasingly constructed to incubate and encourage it. As such, the capacity for the media to affect the way we see the world has never been as broad or as potent.

The Power of Choice

This 21st century phenomenon of such a vast choice when it comes to the information we are exposed to has a profound resonance: we can now, like never before, erase information and content that we don't want to see. We can entirely rid our personal world of it. More than that, social media platforms have an insatiable lust for your information, and social media has a penchant for the tracking of personal info, habits and actions. The impact of these aforementioned characteristics is profound, not least because if you delete a specific post or page from your social media feed, you will then begin to see fewer posts, articles and pages relating to the subject that was the fundamental basis of your angst. With little understanding of the repercussions of your actions- not least the philosophical implications of doing this- and not a care in the world, you have clicked away, prospectively, entire factions of thought, entire quarters of ideological interrogation and influence. In doing this you render yourself increasingly ignorant to the thinkers of these dismissed thoughts, and, more importantly, the reasons that these lines of thought exist.

Take Nigel Farage and UKIP, for example; if you see him pop up, and for whatever reason (legitimate or not so much) decide that you entirely dislike him, you can simply remove the post. Job done. Or, even better, the Facebook savvy amongst us will be assuredly aware of that little drop down menu that allows you to check a box explicitly indicating that you no longer want to see any posts similar to the one that you originally found so disagreeable. Farage and all thinkers like him are gone forever; if any slip through the net, just rinse and repeat. But alas, posts *similar* to the one you deleted/ unfollowed/ whatever'd will *also* begin to appear less and less because of the internet harvesting every single byte of your data and tracking every one of your actions. The very action of ridding your personal news feed of the mother article suggests to the cookies whom haunt our modern existence that you don't just dislike the mother, you dislike the family.

Within this point we establish a new dynamic to the postmodern information monolith that is social media and the data tracking phenomenon: your philosophical and intellectual reality is shaped by social media and its algorithms. Your experiences on social media do this a-consciously; that is to say, neither consciously or unconsciously, and both at the same time. In the conscious decisions you make to shape your experiences, social media is shaping your unconscious perception of the world and the news it bears, because of your unavoidable action of expressing preference and choice. Social media has the supreme power, the sovereign power above all other media which does this, to capture and manipulate this principle. The sinister implication here is that whether or not it does (which, indeed, it unequivocally does) is irrelevant, a moot point, because the fact is that using this principle, social media has the unique power to manipulate data and render the agendas of a few people, and certain ideologies, extremely prevalent, and dangerously enforceable. It would be nice to think it doesn't use it but then, look at the content control actioned by Facebook, Twitter and Google through page control, bans, shadow bans and restrictions and think to yourself: "is there a visible or clear bias here?". You just might be surprised... In any case, the point is that through the magic of social media and the unprecedented scope it affords its users to choose the information they are exposed to, opinions are now being built and reinforced subliminally.

The classic media still does this, but because of its "fixed" nature-meaning that once a newspaper has been published or a program has been made and the advertising agenda and content decided then it cannot be changed- it doesn't have nearly the scope of manipulation nor control that is enjoyed by the flexible neo media, the social media. Social media evolves in real time to cater to the specific audience of one that is the unique user on the platform. No two news feeds will be identical; every newspaper (and for the most part every TV station) is.

It is perhaps interesting that the press has for centuries now been prescribed as the fourth pillar of democracy, after the people, the aristocracy and the clergy no less: the fourth estate. In the context of the 18th century in which that term was coined, one could quite clearly reason with Burke (who first used the term, allegedly) because of the capacity of the press and the press alone to present news and information in a standardised context- Not in an objective or impartial context, but in a *standardised* one. This capacity presented people with an informed understanding of national affairs (mostly political then, as now) to an overwhelmingly enlightening degree.

Part of this enlightening information was possible because of the revolutionary, persistent and key aspect of the press that is the value placed on maintaining a free press, present in Britain as early as the 1690s; not just a press free to report on anything and everything, but, most importantly, free from government influence and penal scrutiny. Balancing governmental intervention and proper conduct is a difficult and ongoing task, but it is one largely left up to the diligence of the judiciary to decide the fate of those deemed to have overstepped the line. Why does this matter in regard to the power of the media? Because with freedom comes choice, and with choice comes power. In the context of conveying information, the modern media has almost *all* the choice and as such, almost all the power.

Crucial to democracy as the access to information is, so too is its dispersal to the masses. With the advent of social media, we are seeing great discrepancies in the dispersal of information and as such huge questions regarding its efficacy in a democracy. For now, it doesn't look like it's going anywhere, though, and as such all media is free to present any argument and any opinion, to criticize religion, politicians, people, monarchy- anyone and anything. They are free to write opinion pieces on anything, anyone and everything, and in the case of online media, manipulate the audience that sees it. They are not necessarily free to manufacture news, or even information *per se*; but with their newfound ability to choose precisely who sees the content they make, the media are free to manufacture *narratives*.

Narratives.

What is a narrative? As described by the OED, a narrative is "a spoken or written account of connected events; a story". What is important here is threefold: specifically, who is writing or speaking, how does one define "connected" and what qualifies something, in the world of politics, as an "event"? Understanding this, one quickly understands the importance of narratives and the power they have over our thoughts, as well as I should hope the features which distinguish a narrative from a news story; news stories can be part of a narrative, and can even form them (Epstein didn't kill himself, Jeremy Corbyn is an anti-Semite etc), but they are not necessarily all that is required to build or produce a narrative; narratives do not by necessity either start or end with news. More often than not, narratives become the news; they are built before they are reported.

For example, eating a bacon sandwich, as an individual event, it is fairly inconsequential- perhaps even unworthy of being called "news"- but as a building block in a *narrative* of awkwardness, inability to speak to the British public and inability to represent the country, a bacon sandwich has the proven potential to be fatal to a prime ministerial hopeful in Britain. As a part of a narrative, a bacon sandwich can in fact be a consequential leviathan. As a part of a narrative, a bacon sandwich has massive potential to develop how we think and perceive the consumer as a person, and, should they be in politics, as a politician. Just ask Ed Miliband.

Narratives are indeed curious things. Imagine the narrative of a major prime ministerial candidate from a major political party, during an election period no less, being focused around a bacon sandwich. Hahhah, imagine. Or better yet, imagine a narrative of swinely sexual misconduct being constructed around a prime minister at the time of crucial election and referendum campaigning. Oh, the obscurity! Surely we would never be reduced to such school yard tomfoolery? Unfortunately, we most certainly were, and are. This begs the question: why would adults of any intellect care about such stories of misconduct or lacking sandwich etiquette? Well, therein lies the power of the media driven narrative, and the power afforded by their ability to choose what kind of narrative they manufacture.

You see, it doesn't matter if you don't care, or if you think it's all lies, or irrelevant rubbish. What matters is that you *are* thinking about it, and as such, that you are *talking* about it. Ed Miliband awkwardly eating a sandwich bears no reflection on his ability to lead a country, not least visible in the fact that it wasn't him and his entire shadow cabinet awkwardly eating the same sandwich. But what it does is present him in an awkward, unrelatable, *unelectable* light. It dehumanises him; I mean, who the bloody hell in modern Britain can't deal with a classic British dietary cornerstone like the bacon sandwich? Not my prime minister, that's for sure. And sure enough, my prime minister he was not, and the impact of "sandwichgate" will never fully be known. What we can speculate upon, however, is the narrative developed upon and around that controversy, and from this we can extrapolate the power of the media.

This is because narratives are essentially bread crumb trails through a forest of events and in using them- or more accurately, developing them- the media is (not even subliminally) trying to guide you through that forest of news and information precisely the way it wants you to go. The left will guide you their way, the right will guide you theirs. What is important to realise is that firstly, the media, in developing these narratives, isn't *necessarily* lying to you or being dishonest- as is often suggested- but is specifically *guiding* your thought processes, your ideological and philosophical foundations and convictions. After all, philosophy is the process of thought based on reason, or the pursuit of reason and understanding through thinking. Therein lies the power of the media, in a concise idiom: it can capture emotion, and harbour fear, anger, animosity, divisions and anguish. If a publication wants to develop and present a narrative of fear, it can and will do so. If a publication or platform wants to paint a political figure as a hero, a saint, a modern-day robin hood, it can do, *and it will.*

Jeremy Corbyn is the perfect subject of this phenomenon, as there are two vastly different narratives being painted of him: one is that he is the working- man- saviour of the British working class, that he is the man to destroy the greedy, nasty Tories and take all the ill-gotten money from the hoodwinking bankers and give it to the poor, lowly, cheated workers. The other, is that he is weak, hates the idea of wealth and meritocratic capitalism, despises business and industry, wants the government to own everything, is going to tax everyone into oblivion, has no idea about economics and as such is destined to throw money at failing public services and plummet the country into economic disrepair. Oh, and the anti-Semite narrative as well... That one is pretty devastating.

So when you're hearing about fake news, or the fact that the Daily Mail is a racist rag that publishes nothing but lies and has no place in the British media, you're often really hearing disagreement with the *narratives* being presented by the Daily Mail. As such, you are looking through a window of modern ideological development and interpretation, shaped by the newspapers and media. Obviously, some of what you read and deem as fake news is in fact falsity being purposely reported as fact, but more often than not, and in an ode to the pitfalls of politics, most things have an element of perception about them, an element of bendable truth, of subjectivity. Most things in politics and society are consequently susceptible- and often fall victim to- the development of narratives.

Truth and "Truth".

Take food banks, as a decent contemporary example: we hear accounts of more than "a million people using foodbanks and rising", that it's a disgrace, that it's crazy how a government can relegate the existence of people to the charity of private citizens. It is, however, not so clear cut, and the "facts" surrounding foodbanks are not so unambiguous. Challenges to those assertions can include many things, such as the observation that foodbank usage statistics are very changeable, and extremely subjective. The Trussell trust website itself saying that the figure of 1.8million is no reference to actual individuals, nor families; It is actually reference to the tokens distributed, many of which are given to people multiple times, meaning the number of actual individuals using them stands to be at least half, probably less. Again, the website itself says that most users are offered tokens twice, on average[24]. Furthermore, the fact that as a society we can support our vulnerable and weak with food tokens is testament to our advancement as a nation and a people- it's probably a safe bet that the circa 400 million Indians living in poverty would relish the idea of foodbanks.

To put it in perspective, 1.8million people is less than 3% of the population taken at face value; less than 1.5% accounting for the aforementioned Trussell Trust considerations (and the assumption that each individual user is given at least two tokens). In context, there are over a million-individual people in the UK earning £100,000 per year. We are a rich country and in the context of global leagues, we are extraordinarily high up the table of poor provisions. But that doesn't matter; how they are portrayed depends on the political narrative that the publications you are reading are trying to build, combined with your ideological predisposition; your willingness to accept the narrative or reject it. Ideology and philosophy are the key factors of this

---

[24]   As   explained   by   the   Trussell   Trust   on   its   website   here: <https://www.trusselltrust.org/news-and-blog/latest-stats/end-year-stats/>

narrative building and are silently etching themselves on the reality and perceptions of the uninitiated.

By "uninitiated", I mean those who are not educated in politics, ideology or philosophy and have no concern with them as disciplines of academia. The kind of people to whom the intricacies of ideology and philosophy are not an everyday consideration; in reality, the vast majority of the population. Those not concerned with the origins of thought, the nuances of terminology or the interrogation of political morality. Those not concerned with the interrogation of phenomenological meaning behind what is said or the words that are used. Those who are not concerned with asking why they can't say or think certain things. More than that, the growing number of pseudo 'intellectuals' who practice the warfare of right and left with little to no knowledge of the real terms implications of the ideological right and left. Taxation- is it theft or the subscription we pay to live in a civilised society? As far as the further right-wing thinker is concerned, taxation is the path to forfeiting one's self- mastery, the path to full state control of the population. As far as the centre-right Tories are concerned, taxation is seldom the answer, and a lot of their broad policy direction reflects this point, such as lowering income taxes and removing the lowest earners from taxation altogether. If it is theft as far as you're concerned, then you are by proxy subscribed to ideological aspects of the classically liberal/ libertarian right, the idea that meritocratic earnings are a reward for realising your potential. If you consider taxation as a justified subscription, then you are leaning towards the interventionist left, redistributed wealth, the idea of a bigger state - in its ultimate manifestation, socialism.

This point also inspires the seldom asked follow up questions- "who is that subscription paid to and why?". In open discussion, it is not rare to see "the government" used synonymously with the "the people"; *we* are the taxpayer, so any public money is *our* money. With the likes of the SNP, they often describe their position as the "voice of Scotland", implying by virtue of this admission that *they* are the vocal outlet for the people of Scotland. Singular, unitary. In truth, the government is an institution with an agenda as much as- if not more than- any private individual or company. Paying taxes is you *paying* the government, who then distribute that money throughout the state. Without a mechanism of taxation, it is actually quite difficult for "the state" to exist at all, and even if it did, not so obvious as to why it would command any respect or authority.

When concerning oneself with nuanced issues such as those mentioned above, it is all too easy to forget that the media seek to commandeer them as their own; they want to become the gatekeepers of these issues, these narratives, dictating not only narrative direction but also guiding potential interpretation. Academic ideological debate is almost futile in such a receptive sea of ignorance and blindness. More than that, the general rule is that people simply do not *care*. People like *consuming* much more than they like *considering*. People can consume much more than they have the capacity, or even the desire, to consider. Media is there to deliver content- social media more so to aggregate it- and consumers are there to consume.

Media is not enjoyable when all you do is meticulously interrogate the philological and phenomenological connotations of every individual word you read, but it is within those areas that the most information is hidden. It is unreasonable to even suggest that people do this; but it is reasonable to suggest that people at least actively, seriously and honestly consider their own intellectual shortcomings when consuming media. This is the suggestion that it isn't reasonable for a fat person to interrogate the precise nutritional value of everything they eat, but to at least acknowledge that anything they eat stands to make them fatter. Don't run or hide from the fact you are fat, acknowledge it. If snacks are enjoyable, the fat person will continue to consume them. If the narrative to which they subscribe is agreeable, the consumer, understood as a personification of all their opinions, perspectives and experiences, will inevitably consume; like the fat person with food, there is nothing objectively wrong with this, but both the fat man and the media consumer ought to understand that their gluttony will bring with it repercussions and ultimately damage them, possibly fatally.

Information saturation does not lead to enlightenment, just like overindulgence in food, no matter how "healthy", does not lead to perfect health. Interesting, then, that whilst the media may well have a pivotal role in developing our moral and political compass, it does not command full control of this role. Indeed, the disciplines of ideology, philosophy and politics and our perceptions thereof are not simply invented or manufactured by the media; they have much wider and deeper tributaries than that.

V
The Political Party.

"*Democracy is a kingless regime infected by many kings.*"- Benito Mussolini

***

There are many measures of ideology within politics, ranging from self-assessment to accepted, consensus, academic definition. Many methods of defining political ideology have their intellectual flaws, but are accepted in their own right for what they are. For example, Benito Mussolini self-defined his nationalistic flavour of communism as fascism[25], whilst Francis Fukuyama quantified western politics en masse- the generally witnessed and broadly post-war-practiced ideals of western liberal democracy- as the "end of ideology"[26]. This assessment gained plenty of critique from the academic world, but, hidden within the intellectual battle royale between thinkers agreeing with the assured statement by Fukuyama and those engaged in the ensuing backlash, it illustrates

---

[25] Outlined in "*the Doctrine of Fascism*" by Mussolini himself. Of course, the word "fascist" has been bastardized into irreverence since.

[26] Fukuyama, F. (2006). *The end of history and the last man: with a new afterword*. New York, Ny Free Press.

---

a vital and forthcoming point: ideology is fluid, not solid or rigid at all. Largely because of this fluidity, Ideology can be manipulated and changed to suit rhetoric (such as with Mussolini and his utilitarian transition from avidly communist to decidedly fascist) or to simply quantify observations of ideological and political progression, as with Fukuyama.

However, ideology is not just fluid; it is also volatile, and this is a problem because volatility is unpredictable. Unpredictability, in politics, is entirely undesirable, even though that it is the permanent state of politics. If politicians could remove all uncertainty and know exactly how an election was going to go, exactly how their term in office would play out policy by policy, and exactly what each policy would do, they would; for all involved life would be easier, and probably a lot more honest. But alas, they can't. What they can do, however, is try to limit that volatility, and it is within this point we begin to witness the lucrative nature of political parties. In limiting the chaos of volatility, they encourage stability afforded order[27]; something political parties adore.

Party Ideology.

Political parties produce this order in an excess of ways, but primarily the chaos they can work to mitigate is the chaos of ideology, that most volatile of human constructions. Political parties have an inextricable, necessary and unavoidable relationship with ideology, and this relationship is perhaps best viewed in this way: ideology is a foundation upon which a political party is built. The party, like any building, can take many different forms and even look entirely different to another iteration of a building built upon the same ideological foundations. One nation Toryism and neoliberal Thatcherism, or Old and New Labour, for example; same foundations, different buildings. This isn't a problem, though. It is merely the case. Political parties, like buildings, can vary enormously in both appearance and function.

The political party is structured such that it offers people with broadly similar goals a singular destination where they can seek to realise those goals. If you are a single ideologue, practising an ideology with extreme virility, it is highly unlikely (if not practically impossible) for you to ever be given a platform upon which you could realistically translate that virility into power and enact

---

[27] Another of the many valuable offerings of Jordan B. Peterson to the world being this idea of chaos and order being mutually exclusive, and in the desirability of order over chaos. A concept which elicits consideration in most, if not all, avenues of life.

change; and change, it must be understood, is always the ultimate goal- however it may look- for all ideologues, just as it is with all political parties. Political parties purposefully cast a wide net because they rely, naturally, on support and numbers. Individuals, conversely, do not cast a broad net because they are not immediately seeking to catch anything; they have their opinions and their perceptions of the world, and they don't ned any wider justification than their own convictions.

The main difference for the political party is that through bringing together individuals, all of whom must sacrifice small, nuanced differences in how they think their chosen ideology should manifest in order to achieve greater goals, the political party broadens its reach and appeal. In broadening its reach and appeal, for all to whom it appeals it offers an increased possibility of becoming the vessel of change that they want to see. Broad reach is, however, both finite and relative, and reliant upon offering a clear message and an obvious ideological and political direction. They encourage members to subjugate their ideological individualism in favour of a shared ideological identity, and the more ideological nuances are sacrificed by individuals within a political party, the more potent the party as a political entity becomes. The more potent a party becomes, the more attractive it becomes to other potential ideologues seeking to implement actionable change; in this way, the successful political party creates a positive feedback loop.

The idea that parties need numbers and people need ideological homes, coupled with the observation that people must become increasingly less precious about their ideological opinions and perspectives the more they want their broader political goals to be realised, ultimately culminates in a political party finding a home in the "centre-ground" when as many nuances as possible have been sacrificed by as many followers as possible to create as broad an appeal as possible. It must be remembered that this culminating in the absolute political centre is not *necessarily* the goal or the reality of individual or specific parties; merely the apex of this phenomenon of ideological nuance sacrifice; its final manifestation, as it were. Like most things in politics, the degree to which *most* political parties achieve or even want this nuance sacrifice exists more on a continuum than a dichotomy. Hence, mainstream parties often end up right or left of centre and rarely, if ever, absolutely centrist.

The centre-ground is a curious beast, especially in the Westminster model of politics, for many reasons. The most perplexing for the free thinker may well be the fact that it attracts the most support but offers the least pronounced change. What specifically does this observation indicate? That people don't have much knowledge of what they want politically, or how it can be achieved? That people are dismally predictable? That ideologically speaking, the most pronounced desires gain the least traction? Probably yes to all, and with regards to the latter the logic is quite easy: the more ideologically pronounced (and as such focused) your goals become, the more friction they create with other thinkers. For example, equality in its broad sense is quite desirable by most people, but as soon as you split the idea of equality into the two factions of "outcome" and "opportunity" you start to divide support. This phenomenon intensifies the more the individual parochialises the definition of what they mean by equality as a concept, until they are rendered voiceless because of lacking or lost support.

Political parties embrace ideologies for the support those ideologies can bring them. They have to distinguish themselves from one another, and they have to look different, but in reality they are looking to appeal to as broad an audience as possible and to do that, they must align with the ideological convictions of as broad an audience as possible. The centre allows them to do this with the most efficacy because the centre-ground harbours and seeks to maintain ideological ambiguity: the bigger the net, the greater the catch.

Weak Minds, Safe Seats.

This ideological proclivity of political parties to play safe and gun for the centre rather than be ideologically bold speaks to another phenomenon rampant in British politics: safe seats. A safe seat is one which a single political party has dominated for such a period of time that it is assumed the seat will go to them unless something radical happens; essentially the modern equivalent of rotten boroughs. The 2019 December election was a good demonstration of the kind of radical exception that would cause safe seat voters to break ranks, and the huge valence issue of Brexit, coupled with a broadly unpopular Labour leadership, was enough for the Labour electorate to lend their votes in their thousands to the Conservatives. Quite quickly, one might be inclined to question the integrity of a political force seeking power first and foremost, and also question the tendency of political parties to gravitate towards the centre-ground. Perhaps it isn't quite the innocuous coincidence of pragmatism they would have us believe it to be.

Safe seats are facilitated in no small part by the first past the post (FPTP) electoral system, with, amongst other things, its insatiable proclivity to narrow British politics down to essentially a two party system; not a system whereby there are only two political parties, but a system which heightens the successes and relevance of two political parties over all others, in our case the Conservatives and Labour. Such is the nature of FPTP that other parties often serve to merely fracture the vote away from the biggest potential challenger to the dominant political party in any given seat; as an electoral system, it forces support to gravitate towards large political powers precisely because of this characteristic. Thusly, whilst Labour has been out of power for over a decade, we are still unlikely to see any calls for electoral reform coming from either of the main beneficiaries of this two-party inclination any time soon, because there remains relevance (and as such power) even in loss in such a system. In 2010, it was speculated that such safe seats accounted for between 364 and 382 of the 650 up for grabs[28], meaning that- in theory- a coalition government could have already been formed prior to the actual election. A powerful and damning idea indeed.

The crucial point of these safe seats is that they are dominantly allocated to centre-ground parties, namely Labour, the Conservatives and (to a lesser extent) the Liberal Democrats; their power and relevance is always essentially secure even before a single vote is cast. Democratically speaking, this could (and should) even be observed as a dangerous symptom of tyranny: not understood as archetypical party tyranny, or tyranny of an individual tyrant, but tyranny of an ideological leaning; *intellectual* tyranny of ideology. The kind of tyranny in fact, that goes completely unnoticed, because of the passive reception it has enjoyed by the electorate and the population on the whole, under the guise of being voted for and "supported" by a system dressed a lot like what we expect democracy to look like. The kind of tyranny that produces an Orwellian, panopticon[29] style state of political existence within a nation. The worst kind of tyranny is that which goes unnoticed; this- the ideological centre-ground and the opportunist political party- is a contender for that crown.

More than that, the political centre-ground creates an atmosphere within which you, as an individual, must adhere to this ideological tyrant- adhere to the doctrine of western liberal democracy (WLD)- or become a social pariah. Adhere to the concepts championed by the WLD centrist dogmatists, and their interpretations of them, or face a future of political ostracisation. This ostracisation applies whether you are straying to the left or the right; if you do not follow the dominating ideology of the safe-seat-centrist-postmodern-liberal-

---

28 Depending on where you look. The Electoral reform society was as measured and concise a definition and analysis as I thought necessary, available at: <https://www.electoral-reform.org.uk/the-scourge-of-tactical-voting/>

29 As a concept originally coined by Jeremy Bentham, excellently utilised, discussed and explored by Foucault, M., 1977. *Discipline & Punish*. New York: Pantheon Books.

dogmatists, you might as well consider yourself relegated from the realm of political relevance; your voice will likely never be more audible than a whisper. This is an extremely dangerous intellectual atmosphere to find ourselves in, and it perniciously bleeds into our wider life. The rules it outlines begin to govern everything, not least critical thinking, and taint our world view in accordance with centrist totalitarian dogmatism.

Jeremy Corbyn tried shifting Labour to the further left under an unapologetically socialist, old-old labour manifesto. This cost him and will continue to cost Labour for as long as the shift persists, regardless as to whether he is at the helm or not. Centrist ideology adopted by political parties has manufactured an environment in which, as an essential matter of necessity, you have to play by its rules, and this is a complete usurping of what politics should actually be.

Dialogue and discourse are shut down and limited by the fact in western countries that we have to adhere to the WLD vocabulary and their prescribed meanings. If we want to talk about gender, race or sexuality we must talk about them in a way that the western liberal centre-ground would approve of. If we don't, the conversation is shut down and the participant "cancelled". This is a fundamentally *wrong* way to conduct our political business. Political parties should not be the gatekeepers to philosophy, ideology or power, they should merely be vessels of achieving and implementing those things. We, the citizens, should be the gatekeepers, and it is centrism, with its *de facto* broad appeal, coupled with politicians' lust for power and the peoples' lust for tribal representation, that has made it so we are not. Safe seats encourage political parties to magnify fears, minimise difference and perpetuate the system we are all a part of to solidify their relevance and influential position.

Dubious Ethics.

Political parties nowadays have this ghastly arrogant aura surrounding them whereby, from entry level (grassroots) to the very top (leadership), they seemingly expect you to work for them, and to adopt the mission of simply achieving power specifically for them. The idea goes that if you want change, or more precisely if you want a certain ideology to gain power and change the nation (and potentially the world) somewhere along the lines you see philosophically fit and agreeable, then you have to make some of those previously discussed nuanced sacrifices of your own ideological dogmatism, and you have to use your vote to ascend the closest possible party to your perfect ideological reality into number 10. This is again, fundamentally *wrong*. This principle holds our votes ransom, it holds our ethics and our convictions ransom; it holds our minds ransom and renders them placid and tamed. More importantly than that, it coerces people into passively forgoing their own ethics and convictions for the false and conflated goal of ascending a political party to power. Party politics makes ideology about power, not change.

If the media passively, subconsciously and implicitly shapes the individual's world view, then the political party does it overtly, consciously, and explicitly. The political party feeds on this exact principle; as a concept the political party exists precisely because of it. The political party should not be understood as a road to change, as so often it is sanctimoniously sold as being; it should be understood as a battalion of soldiers marching towards power, led by their officers and generals, with the intention first and foremost of conquest, of usurping power. The *potential* to enact change comes only by default, after the ultimate goal has been realised.

This is to say that the political party as an institution is a monolith, a singular fixed point in the landscape of western liberal democratic life, particularly the long-established political landscape of the UK. What political parties look like -whether that be left, right, centre or otherwise- is necessarily irrelevant when contrasted with the much more impactful question of "what purpose do political parties serve?", the latter question being one which has managed to evade much serious scrutiny for the last century or so. Outside of single-issue parties and their obvious ideological direction and goals, what purpose *does* a political party serve to achieve? Specifically, what purpose does the political party serve to achieve beyond simply acquiring power for itself? Those questions are not so clear cut. For example, couldn't it be argued that parliament could reach quite amicable decisions between 650 MPs all voted in on merit by 650 individual constituencies? Couldn't it also be argued that in removing the easy, tribal party affiliation from parliamentary candidates, we would encourage people to become more politically aware and perhaps even involved? And couldn't it be argued that parliament would be much more democratic without the partisan limitations such as the three-line whip? I certainly think it could.

More interesting is what happens when centrist political parties have that power. More often than we generally care to admit, this amounts to pretty much always more of the same; centrism has locked politics into an ideological monotony. Centrism has a vested interest in preserving centrism, and as such has a natural aversion to actual distinct or marked change. Taxes go reservedly up or down, spending goes reservedly up or down, the NHS, education, social provisions and the economy are always the number one concerns, and they are always addressed under the presumptions of WLD morality. To highlight this, I would simply suggest that you would never see any political party ever pursue an agenda of making education *less* accessible. You might even shudder at the concept, but our perceptions of this idea have been entirely shaped by the WLD "end of ideology" and as such, so too have our reactions; the proposal of making education less accessible will always be met with vehement opposition; it might even be impossible now to make the case at all. Not impossible to present a convincing case for doing so, but impossible to *make it* anywhere in the WLD world. The WLD political party is more an agent of stagnation- intellectual, moral, cultural and political stagnation- than change. Stagnation is repetition, and in repetition the status quo is preserved; to the ideological centrist, the status quo is king.

We have seen ourselves arrive at a world whereby asking philosophical questions which challenge the status quo is increasingly seen as *wrong*. This should frighten anyone who is concerned with freedom in any context whatsoever. The road this takes us down ends with a political atmosphere that makes China look like a bastion of democracy. Does this sound like an overly extreme comparison? Well, let's put it to the test. Let's see how far we have to go to get to something we can't or *shouldn't* say or think, and that if a modern political party in the west hoped to ever gain power, that *they* could not say or think. What about all women shortlists for electoral candidates? Fine? Well, it's not just fine, it happens. What, then, about all *male* candidates? Slightly less tolerable, but not outright intolerable? What about, changing a single word from the acceptable original statement, all *white* candidates? Well, that wasn't very hard.

Upon even seeing the suggestion of all male or all white candidate shortlists, the immediate reaction is one, in some way shape or form, of negativity- animosity, horror, disgust; whatever that negativity might look like. If any party were to suggest all white shortlists, they would surely be lampooned into oblivion by other, more ideologically acceptable (WLD centrist) political parties and mainstream media outlets. This isn't *of itself* a problem; establishing passive parameters of policy serves, amongst other things, to limit extremism from all sides. But the fact that public discourse is now so limited that we are not supposed to even question *why* anymore, and that positions are so often presumed as self-evident, is a catastrophe for our capability and scope to freely think.

We have seen ideology dissolved, by the powers that be, in the caustic solution that is the political party, and as such by proxy we have seen philosophy- the practice of critical thought and consideration- devalued. Any deviance to the WLD centrist status quo is met with vexatious challenge, across the ostensibly varied political aisle, whether that be deviance to policy or thinking.

Coming back to our example of making education less accessible, If one were to for a moment consider the art of debate as best practiced when both parties adopt the concept and position of *charitable debate*- that is, to assume whatever your opponent is saying or arguing is being argued or postured from the most logical, best- possible- meaning stance, and should be interpreted that way before producing a counter position- then, through that charitable lens, is there truly no scenario whereby making education *less* accessible could benefit society? *Truly, none?*

The Power of Compromise.

Political parties, in their unrelenting pursuit of power, media spin and savvy appearance, have been the criminal master minds behind this narrowing of perception; their formulation was based around the idea of realising common goals and taming the chaotic and unpredictable beast of ideology, their proliferation has been based around their unique capacity- and desire- to limit it. They have been aided with this in no small part by the media, and the previously discussed power of the narrative; all ideological persuasions have a media and social narrative, and the elusive gift of having the ability to control that narrative is power incarnate; a power that no political party in the west has yet captured individually, but a power that WLD centralism as an ideology captured decades ago.

For this reason, the political party, as a concept, can be described as the home of ideological compromise, the extent of that compromise predicting that party's electability, a principle culminating in the aforementioned safe seat phenomenon. The party is therefore an agent of relationship between individuals and groups of individuals. The natural question here would be: what, then, would the best relationship between a party and an individual look like? What should the party do for the individual and conversely, what should the individual do for the party? The main consideration at this point should be as follows: what both the individual without the party and the party without the individual look like. Very quickly, considering these two ideas, the value metric of both party and individual is revealed as heavily skewed towards the individual, who has an infinitely larger scope of importance to the party than the party ought to have to the individual. The individual can work with others towards an end goal or objective without flying any particular flag, *per se.* If it came to it, individuals could rally behind one another to enact change.

cooperation does not have to be done under the banner of a political party; it is made *easier* by doing it this way, but the party is not essential to the individual at all.

Contrast this with the political party. She is nothing at all without individual members and supporters. The political party is essentially nothing more than an ideological brand name; it is not necessary to achieve any of the goals that the political party, as a concept, achieves, all of which are at their core merely exhibitions of cooperation between individuals, to varying degrees of intensity. The political party is an expendable concept; the individual is not. This makes the fact that we are so often faced with political parties ideologically void of anything but a desire for power, and so banal as to seek our approval based upon nothing more than our more pronounced *disapproval* for their competition, seem almost satirical. No wonder apathy is drowning participation in this country. The individual has found himself in a world whereby the political party sells itself as a necessity and commands his support as capital towards gaining power. The whole game of politics when it is presented along the paradigm of party politics is a game of power; a constant pursuit for, and lust after, power. It is sport for ideology and philosophy. Political parties are merely the teams playing.

This concept posits, by necessity, that highly pronounced ideology is unlikely to manifest itself in mainstream western politics any time soon (in such a way as to secure any meaningful power). Indeed, we have unfortunately seen over the course of the 20th century what can happen at the extreme ends of the ideological spectrum, and as such perhaps tend to relegate those ideologically virulent parties to the lower leagues- where they occasionally pick up councillors or even more occasionally, regional mayors- with no true capacity to realistically gain power, so long as the tangled and complex party political paradigm is maintained. Whilst perhaps this account has been sceptical, or even scathing, until now, hopefully this paragraph elucidates a key element of centrist party politics that might be worth preserving.

The general population are sceptical and wary of Ideological dogmatism at either extreme end of the political spectrum for a multitude of reasons, and as such often approach increasingly proliferating party ideology with a practiced caution and trepidation. Generally, those ideologues concerning themselves with intensifying ideological position are abrasive, reactionary and erratic. Coupled with that, people have seen over the last 100 years that extreme "left/ right" ideological dogmatism ultimately manifests itself in death, destruction, decay and war. Why is this? Why is it that potent ideology manifests itself in what we could categorise simply and bluntly as "conflict"?

At the face of it the answer might be fairly simple: if animosity, which is expectedly and always felt between two fundamentally opposed ideologues, is allowed to develop and develop *ad infinitum,* then the natural emotional and physical conclusion to be reached is conflict and hatred. Hatred is one of the two most powerful emotions, the other being love; men since the dawn of civilised time have been uniquely willing to fight, kill and die for that which they hate and for that which they love. These are extremes, of action, emotion and reaction. Extremes are how the volatility of ideology finally, ultimately manifests itself. Extremes are how raw ideology, in its final form, has to be realised in order to enact its perfect vision of change; extremes are the end of the road.

Suddenly, the sanctuary of the political party, when viewed through the lens of its capacity to dilute ideological dogmatism, can be witnessed as not just a sanctuary from individual responsibility, but a sanctuary from extremes. In having to make multiple concessions and sacrifice ideological dogmatism for cooperation, support and ultimately, potential power, one has to move away from the extremes. Even Jeremy Corbyn with his old-old-Labour 2019 manifesto of "radical" change and socialism was only really radical when viewed through the lens of western liberal democratic ideals and consensus. To the ideological extremes, it didn't go anywhere near as far as it could have[30].

The centre-ground has, in this sense, a tight monopoly on power, and for a party, power is often motivation in itself, not really an avenue to change. The politician this principle breeds- in a *de facto* sense, the politician that centrist ideology breeds- and the politic this principle encourages exponentially gravitate towards the centre, creating in this cycle a positive feedback loop, whereby centrism becomes more profitable and valuable the more people grasp and hold on to it. We have thusly arrived in the 21st century at a point where centrism is legally well fortified in terms of established practices, institutions, procedures and norms; it is a perfect concept to those looking stabilise all the conflict politics attracts and create an atmosphere able to sustain a career in politics.

The idea of a "career" in politics is a strange one. What do we think of when we think of a career? Stability? Progression opportunities? A pension? Industry influence? Competition? Management? Whatever we think of a career, we ought not to include positions of elected office in our considerations. As far as ideology is concerned, and as far as good politics is concerned, a "career"

---

30 A difficult assertion to make based on the subjectivity, explored within this account, of ideological definition, but one I firmly stand by.

should never include becoming an MP. A civil servant maybe, but never an elected official. Becoming an MP should be more closely understood- and observed in practice- as a duty. Centrism in this light is revealed as much more complex a concept than merely that of an ideological one. It is a concept which facilitates the monopolisation of power and simultaneously offers to bestow it upon individuals; centrism has something to give which many people desire to have; centrism is a reliable supply of power to the insatiable demand. Politics ought not be the place for career minded individuals to nestle in and establish a cushty, well paid tenure of influence and power. Politics ought to be much more complex than that.

Sadly, this is not the case, abetted in no small part by the traditionally powerful position that being a member of parliament has been. One should not have the scope in a democracy- which professes and champions the weight of the individual's vote, no less- to confidently assign themselves a decades long career as a member of parliament. Politicians should not have the leverage of a permanent position of influence to offer when negotiating things, neither in a professional nor a personal capacity. All speculations of parliamentary corruption aside, the potential for an individual to be corrupted in such a position strikes incredibly true; power is one's ability to offer something that no one else can offer, to someone who wants something they cannot otherwise have. If a political party can secure safe seats to anyone, regardless of ideology, regardless of their being an actual member of the community they are supposed to represent, regardless of their stance on fishing in a Cornish constituency, or farming in a Yorkshire one, they can in essence remove real choice and real influence from the voter. To have a system that can give a career to a politician is to have a system that functionally thrusts apathy upon the electorate- and even to some degree compels it.

For these reasons, ideological conviction is more often than not the political pathway to friction, conflict and disappointment. The system is geared to make it obsolete. The uncodified nature of the UK constitution has allowed centrism to secure a vice grip on our political systems, institutions, people and parties. For a potent contemporary example, we can surely observe the successes and failures of UKIP under ex-leader Nigel Farage. Even upon gaining significant support, the system was weighted heavily against them[31], but also evidenced in everything from the amount of time it took to gain any serious traction, the contrast between their EU electoral support and their UK support,

---

[31] Illustrated here: < https://www.bbc.co.uk/news/election/2015/results>

and in the vitriol Farage was met with every time he made any public appearance. However, within the curious case of UKIP the political party, at this juncture, can be observed as not only the best way to secure almost any political change for the individual, as well as political order for the collective, but in many ways, the *only* way.

UKIP was a single-issue party to the core. Sure, they had a few manifestos and presented tepid positions in other areas like non-European migration, law an order, educational discipline etc, but the everything for UKIP was its position on leaving the EU. Though it fell victim to the Westminster centrist bias in almost every national electoral campaign they ever fought, not least in 2015, UKIP has been perhaps the most successful political force in modern UK political history; certainly, post Thatcher. The interesting thing about this, is that for all the barriers in the way of third and fringe parties, and for all the aforementioned flaws of our parliamentary system, precisely the fact that we do engage with party politics is enough to make them valuable. How much more difficult would Brexit have been, in all its glory, if those pushing for it and presenting the arguments had to do so as fractured, individual voices? Immeasurably, and perhaps it would have even been impossible to achieve without the political party unit. Political parties do have the immutable ability to unify minds behind policies that otherwise would likely remain simple whisperings of individualist philosophy.

This suggests the main basis for supporting party politics and gives us an inclination as to the ideological hierarchy of politics in general. Ideas need a pathway to become realities as well as a mechanism to do so. Whilst individuals may each take positions on seemingly incompatible issues, political parties encourage those incompatible positions to remain the preserve of your own philosophy, and make you choose that which you value most. They force us to produce a hierarchy of our philosophical thoughts and, when we compromise on them, facilitate cooperation. Political parties attract broad support because of the order they bring by mitigating the chaos of pronounced, conflicting, individual ideas.

The Party Leader

It is within this profitable compromise, and members' interest in preserving their chosen party and its position of power, that a member- an individual- usually leaves their own politics, ideology, and convictions at the door. When it comes to it, almost always will members vote with the party regardless of their own convictions; even if they won't vote with it, they are extremely unlikely to vote *against* it. The whole Brexit scenario was a superb illustration of this principle in practice, and also a good illustration of what will happen to a member who votes against their party[32]. The members do not distort the party line, they unconditionally adhere to it, and if they do disagree with the party line, they find another avenue to vent their frustrations. This other avenue often takes the form of attacking leadership, where members choose to specifically oppose the leader instead of the party as an institution, as we saw with the perpetual challenge to Jeremy Corbyn's leadership and the stumbling of members to find something- or someone- to blame the catastrophic 2019 election defeat on. Members don't like to attack the party, and seldom will. To do so is to create uncertainty, to challenge the one constant that has afforded them all power, to create chaos within the party and the political landscape, and weaken it to a potentially fatal extent.

Preservation of the party is the goal for most members, perhaps above achieving any specific political goal, as, like we have discussed, without the former there is little hope for the latter. The desire to preserve the party is enough for parties on the whole, as a concept, to have naturally been preserved as institutions and to have stood the trying tests of time for centuries. Political parties render themselves necessary in a self-perpetuating cycle of power lust, acquisition, loss and change. They are the last stand for the would-be democrat against tyranny, understood as old money totalitarianism, not the passive tyranny of ideology that we in the west are currently languishing in. Through all this preservation, however, It is imperative that parties have *changeable* elements if they are to persist through change; rigidity is fragility, and fragility is uncertainty. The political party needs some elements of changeability in order to survive (otherwise how would they ever be able to adapt?), and the most obvious, flexible and useful of these elements is the party leader.

The ideology of the party is developed explicitly, at least in part, by the *leader's* vision of where the party should go, particularly visible in the tenure of Thatcher and the leadership of Corbyn because of how they shifted the status quo of their respective party ideologies when they assumed power. Members "challenging" the party are, in fact, very often members more specifically challenging the leader and *their* ideology or mandated ideological direction; remember, members by virtue of their membership acknowledge by default the

---

[32] With the vote to trigger article 50 passing whilst dozens of MPs opposed it, and the removal of the whip from the Tory MPs who voted to essentially seize control of parliamentary business from Johnson in 2019.

importance of their party and its survivability. If we understand ideology as the foundation, and the party as the building, then the leader is the site foreman; the main man (or woman) building the party structure.

To exemplify this point, a convenient example has presented itself over recent years, in the official stance of the Labour party under Corbyn on trident renewal and the sentiments of Corbyn himself on the subject; the official party line is to have trident[33] [34]. Corbyn himself, however, was extremely vocal and absolute in his anti-nuclear sentiment, specifically his anti-trident sentiment, and as such came under further fire from many of his so called "Blairite" back benchers and even members of the shadow cabinet. What we have here, is a unique window into the developments and role of ideology within a party, unlike anything we have witnessed in 21st century British politics; there was so much conflict, animosity and challenge between everyone in Corbyn's Labour from the grassroots to the lords, yet Corbyn himself appears to be the one factor that simultaneously adheres the party to any support it has received since his tenure as leader, as well as any lost support or condemnation it has received in the same period. It has largely been directed towards, and accredited to, just the man himself, not the 'Labour party'; at most, "Corbyn's Labour".

Even the rifts and the internal conflicts in Labour had been argued as directly his fault, directly his responsibility, not just as the leader but as the ideological beacon and ambassador of the party. Labour was then Corbyn centric- inextricably tied to Corbyn, as the Conservatives throughout the '80s were to Thatcher- and this infamy will reign long after his stepping down, a magnified Enoch Powell phenomenon. In an ode to Powell, if Corbyn leaves, he will almost certainly take his support with him[35] as his replacement was always destined to be a centrist or a "moderate"; if it wasn't- if for example Rebecca Long- Bailey had won, then there was a damn good chance of some dubious tension and maybe even a Labour party split. The electorate then, it could be suggested, are voting for the ideology *he* professes and the man *he* is portrayed

---

[33] Evidenced here in 2017: <https://www.theguardian.com/politics/2017/apr/23/jeremy-corbyn-casts-doubt-labour-support-trident-nuclear-deterrent-manifesto>

[34] And here in 2019 as the saga continues: <https://www.theguardian.com/politics/2019/nov/25/labours-progressive-manifesto-let-down-by-stance-on-trident>

[35] For an enlightening and excellent insight into exactly this phenomenon I would direct you, with an open mind, towards "Lewis, R. (1979). *Enoch Powell: principle in politics.* London: Cassell"

s, not the party. They are voting- or not voting-for Corbyn, not Labour. They re rejecting Corbynism, not the Labour party itself, precisely because it seems ke Labour has adopted Corbynism and in doing so, rejected all important ompromise.

But perhaps that borders too much on the speculative, and offers a omewhat banal overtone to my point, which is this: the political party is an deological leviathan. It can offer the member freedom from the confides of iscovering and developing their own personal ideology, freedom from the icklustre endeavour of delivering and pushing one's own personal message of deology and political philosophy, and freedom from having to gain a following nd support without any pre-established electable credentials or academic nerit in the process. It offers the ability to achieve *power*, and that in itself is nough to entrap (dare I say most) people into its leviathan jaws.

Political parties are rivers, carving their way through a canyon of deological stone. Seemingly a valiant action plagued with difficulty; but yet, the arty, like the river, always takes the path of least resistance. Whilst it might eem that the party is fighting for a cause with honour and purpose, in reality it s just trying to keep flowing; for it is within the act of flowing that the party ltimately has the chance to reach the sea of power. All parties seek power like ll rivers seek the seas. It is important to recognise that rivers, like political arties, do this as a matter of procedure, not as an act of triumph; they wat the ewards, they seek the power. Just because the journey might seem difficult oes not mean that it's admirable or virtuous as a matter of fact. Political arties capture the wants of people and like the poisoned apple to snow white, ffer a delicious sweet solution based upon perceived desires.

As a member, you don't have to be academically astute, freethinking or ritical. All that you have to do is support the party, no matter what. The party lows, and you go with that flow. More than that, because of the faction fetish ve have historically had, still have and will continue to have as the Aristotelian, nperfect humans we are and are destined to forever remain, political parties owadays don't even need to offer any solutions to any problems other than he "problem" of other parties. The simple threat of losing is enough to drive nost to want to win. The warfare is done symbolically. Policy, philosophy, deology and even character are on the backburner of critique, trumped by the asy emotional capital generated by the faction battle in the perpetual party- olitical conflict. You vote Tory because you *don't* want Labour, and vice versa. olitical parties give you a team; all you have to be is a team player.

VI
Universal Manipulability.

"Because to take away a man's freedom of choice, even his freedom to make the wrong choice, is to manipulate him as though he were a puppet and not a person."- Madeline L'Engle

***

Politics and politicians rely on the fact that people and their thinking are malleable. *Everyone* is susceptible to ideological and philosophical manipulation in some capacity, and all of the aforementioned phenomena illustrate some of the different weapons and methods at the disposal of a would-be manipulator. Political parties regularly organise this manipulation both publicly and overtly, through things like official party lines and faction-based, adversarial opposition. Many methods of manipulation are subtle, like the subliminal news feed and the passive influence of personal circles- the loudest and most vocal of your friends will often be the voice of *most* of your friend group's political persuasion. This whole exposé isn't particularly news in itself, so why is it relevant? Because it is precisely the principle that politicians (amongst other professionals, such as advertising marketers and journalists) try to capture.

These people are not so much trying to manipulate you, as is so often argued the case, but more that they are simply appealing to your manipulability, that's all. They are relying on your *potential* susceptibility to the rhetoric of their message, and on the *potential scope* to win followers. The potential for you to be manipulated is all that is necessary for these forces; their messages and soundbites are tailored to that principle- they do not create it. All of these different people are presenting something which we ought to know is for sale and they're simply trying to entice us into buying it. Your potential to be manipulated is money- they're trying to earn it, not print it. The susceptibility to manipulation was there long before the rhetoric developed by these people to tap into it; without that susceptibility, manipulative rhetoric would be useless- it would serve literally no purpose. The fact that we often remain ignorant to our lacking intellectual fortifications- ignorant to the ease with which we can be manipulated- is what gives the practice so much power.

To manipulate is to exercise power. Manipulation in an interpersonal context is by its very nature the act of making someone do something (included in this is to make them "think" something) that without your influence, or the influence of what you can promise, they otherwise would not do. Manipulation is not exclusively as overt as it is with political parties, nor is it always negative or odious; your manager at work is manipulating you into working with the promise of money, and whilst at work, he is manipulating your behaviour with the threat of disciplinary action. Of course, we don't tend to view this relationship as one of manipulation, because it's mutually agreed upon via the signing of a contract and in many ways, mutually beneficial. But it must be known that, by definition, the exercise of controlling a situation for a desired outcome *is* manipulation.

In such obvious but not so immediately apparent cases as the worker and the manager, our readiness to accept manipulation is visible. When manipulation is viewed through the lens of raw definition, it is revealed as what must surely be a regular, daily breach of our minds' fortifications. This idea audibly (if a little controversially, perhaps) resonate with Aristotle's notions of slave and master as outlined in *Politics*[36] in so far as it suggests we are regularly involved in situations where we are powerless and others are exerting power over us. It also presents to us an insight that hopefully allows us to transcend the misapprehension that we are masters of our own minds, and through the earthquake of anecdotes allows us to peer into the now open fissures that are

---

[36] Aristotle, Saunders, T.J. and Sinclair, T.A. (1982). *Aristotle: the politics*. Middlesex: Penguin. Aristotle suggests that people are predisposed to be either slaves or masters, to be the powerful or the powerless. He does not necessarily see this as a bad thing but acknowledges as a matter of necessity that it is, indeed, a thing.

the profound ways in which, to reiterate my opening sentiment, we are *all* susceptible to manipulation in some way; we are all, universally, manipulable.

A sentiment with such dangerous scope as this will always attract dangerous thinkers; psychopaths and sociopaths, murderers and rapists- some of the worst society has to offer. Though, on the other side of the same coin, it will also attract the best and brightest- when a scientist tells you about string theory or supernovas, or the Higgs Boson, they are trying to *manipulate* your thoughts *into* understanding. Again, I want the reader to be fully aware that I do not think this principle is intrinsically negative in any way, shape or form. In fact, I would posit that it is an ultra-nihilistic idea, one which bestows no allegiance to any definition of good nor evil; simply, that it is afforded by the natural human condition and is a matter of ambivalent fact.

From Opinion to Fact, and Back Again.

Our intrinsic, natural potential to be manipulated, and our susceptibility to manipulation, are principles that we should *all* be aware of if we are to even flirt with the idea of engaging in measured and informed discussion surrounding political, philosophical and ideological issues. In general, we are reluctant to accept this -our openness to manipulation- and nor do we accept its culpability in the forming of our opinions. Some of the most relevant and obvious illustrations of this point evidence themselves politically in "toxic issues", such as the NHS, social welfare, and race relations; in the fact that there are issues which completely elude any sort of rational debate beyond certain paradigms, certain boundaries of discussion. We cannot practically talk about these things unless the content of our words falls within certain acceptable positions.

Liberalism, in one form or another, dominates the British political landscape, and as such those certain conditions of discussion are easily observable in modern British politics: talk about the NHS, but do not talk about *privatising* the NHS. Talk about social welfare, but do not talk about altogether *removing* social welfare. Talk about race, but do not talk about race indicating culture. Whether any of the above positions are right, wrong or stupid doesn't matter, because they illustrate a forthcoming point: our political leaders and those seeking power will never publicly mention certain opinions at all, and certain perspectives are not even possible to express should you wish to have any political or even public electoral success. By extension of this, these opinions become extremely difficult to hold, and are conditioned out of the public sphere of discussion by the very fact that they are toxic. These issues are completely void of any real *debate*, in favour of simple, safe *discussion*.

Discussion is not debate, and the two can be easily mistaken for each other. More than that, discussion can be seamlessly disguised as debate. Discussion is conversation, generally limited conversation, around specific topics whereby the people discussing them have broadly similar positions. Debate, on the other hand, involves at least two people with different positions on the same subject offering their perspective and challenging the other. Political discussion is conducive only to the egos of those supporting what is being discussed; debate gives a voice to those *opposing* as well as supporting the opinion at hand. A debate only starts when an opposing opinion is introduced and allowed airtime. And yet, toxic issues are always rendered mundane, predictable, ultimately useless discussions in the aura of manipulated rhetoric and discourse that tends to surround them. This is Orwellian control of ideas being exhibited, and it is exhibited most masterfully by specifically one group of people: politicians.

Politicians are perhaps the most dangerous group of all that capture and utilise the idea of universal manipulability, because of their unique authority in shaping our perceptions and understanding of ideology and philosophy, two subjects on which we are, as a population, sorely undereducated. From a young age, we are conditioned into the norm by the opinions of the educators and institutions we spend our first eighteen years perpetually absorbing. We are then released into life with a greater understanding of chlorofluorocarbons and polymers than epistemology, the difference between empiricist and rationalist thinkers, the teachings of John Locke or even who Socrates was and why he was important.

We have an intermediate understanding (in theory, the plight of British education notwithstanding) of nuclear physics when we leave high school- an understanding of the mechanics and theory behind atomic bombs, nuclear power and the relevance of atomic half-life- and yet most of us leave even college with zero academic understanding of philosophy or ideology, the foundations of the political parties or the implications of their manifestos. If it was the business of educational institutions to provide us with a basic understanding of these subjects, the discourse on things like privatisation of the health services would no doubt change drastically. But sadly, it isn't, and as such the burden of persuasion damningly falls on politicians and political commentators, probably the last people we should have in such a position.

There perhaps wouldn't be any problem with the amount of power this position affords in the hands of this select and extremely specific group of people if their intentions were pure, but unfortunately, they rarely (if ever) are. Politicians give interviews with *their* reputations in mind, *their* careers; they offer *information* with the same considerations. Political commentators do precisely the same thing, a phenomenon exhibited daily in all branches of the media, and uniformly we can witness this culminating in one the generation of one thing: argument. Whether the HuffPost is arguing for a second EU referendum (again), the Sun is arguing against Islam, or the BBC is arguing over gender pay gaps, arguments are flourishing and perpetual.

The problem with this, and how this anomalous paragraph ties in with the idea of universal manipulability, is that arguments bear no intellectual fruit, because the very essence of argument- separate from 'debate'- relies upon tired, rotten ideas and subjects to inspire *emotion*, not thought. A sentiment captured well by Edward de Bono in *I am Right You Are Wrong*[37] in which the fundamental flaw of argument is suggested as being its propensity to encourage an individual to pursue his desire to *prove himself right*, not broaden his understanding, nor indeed the academic depth, of the subject being argued. Rock logic over water logic; intellectual rigidity over intellectual fluidity.

Consequently, and particularly within the fields of politics, ideology and philosophy, we have a broad and general lack of understanding surrounding the subjects themselves because they are constantly delivered to us dishonestly, with an agenda in mind, through the medium of either discussion (no conflicting opinion) or argument (ignorant and bigoted aggressive positions). Coupled with the usual gravitation we have towards sources of information that we have already committed to liking, trusting and enjoying, not only are we rendered susceptible to subjective information presented as fact (misinformation), but also, we are emotionally prepared to accept and follow the mood and tone of what is being presented. This absence of critical thinking, afforded by our distinct lack of understanding, renders us, universally, manipulable.

But there is more to the story than pure ignorance; indeed, one's capacity to be manipulated doesn't begin *or* end with ignorance. A strong understanding and knowledge of a subject can be met with an acceptance of manipulation- scholars in their subject fields are manipulated regularly by conflicting evidence and accounts within them. Eluding full circle to the idea of the employee and the employer, I would suppose that most wouldn't categorize completing daily tasks for pay as manipulation, but indeed, it is- it is the practice of allowing individuals to influence your behaviour in ways you would otherwise not behave in. We are all manipulable, and it happens to us *daily,* across all faucets of our lives, not just in politics. Political manipulation is, however,

---

37 Edward De Bono (2016). *I am right, you are wrong: from this to the new renaissance: from rock logic to water logic.* London: Penguin Life. (Pp.7)

particularly nefarious, because of its unique scope to affect more than just your actions and force you into decisions and situations you are poorly qualified to engage with.

Brexit (and Emotional Capital).

Brexit has been a good contemporary example of this- in the cacophony of hollow rhetoric and noxious argument by politicians and commentators on both sides, we have been rendered an electorate with collectively little knowledge of what we actually voted for (again, on both sides), and suffered under a succession of governments with zero idea what they're doing, who were effecting whatever they were doing with alarmingly efficient inadequacy, an opposition calling for everything from a Brexit U-turn and a second referendum to a general election and a vote of no confidence, and political commentators, journalists and online personalities losing their vision of Brexit in the white noise that is entirely ignorant dialogue.

You want £350 million a week for your NHS? Vote leave. Simple as that. You want to avoid economic catastrophe? Vote remain, and whilst you're at it, mock the leave voters. There was, as is sadly very often the case, little to no philosophical discourse within Brexit, no discourse designed to educate and inspire *understanding* as to the repercussions of this grand and valiant decision. Sure, we were told that the Brexit will cost thousands of jobs, that the IMF suggested an economic recession immediately after a Brexit vote, this select committee said British manufacturing was going to all but dissolve in the wake of Brexit, that select committee said British farming would cease to exist post Brexit. But we were very seldom told *why* these conclusions had been met, save for the occasional filibuster about percentage increases in production, taxation, labour cost; this and that. It was one big argument, with the agenda of securing agreement, not enlightenment. "Agree with me because…". The whole Brexit fiasco was a waltz of misinformation, of emotional, political and economic manipulation.

Brexit also highlighted the uncomfortable truth that universal manipulability is a concept which people don't like to admit exists, similar in principle to how people will or will not admit they have biases, dependent upon how socially desirable or undesirable those biases supposedly are. To suggest that you, as an individual, are not just easy to manipulate, but are constantly being manipulated, is to reduce life and consciousness down to the whims of the powerful and strong. Maybe it is, and in concluding that the "powerful and strong" exist we must also accept that we are implying that the "powerless and weak" exist; we must accept that if someone is manipulating then there must be someone being manipulated. And we must accept that we are potentially, at any given point, either the former or the latter, and perhaps more often one than the other.

In any situation, you may be the powerful manipulating party or the weak, manipulated party. When asking for a discount on a hairdryer at the local store you are the powerful manipulator; after all, they want to make the sale. When the store clerk says you can have it but only if you take out an extended warranty to protect your purchase, you suddenly become the weak manipulated. It can change just that quickly. Salesmen will likely tell you that everyone has a price, and we truly do. There is a figure or promise anyone could give to have you do anything; to establish what that is, simply start absurd and work your way down to the least absurd price you will take. To drive your car on the wrong side of the road I might offer you £100, and you'd perhaps say no- the risk far outweighs the reward. What if I offered £100 billion? Would it still be a no? If not, then what about £100 Million? £100,000? £10,000? You start at the absurd and work down. For almost everything there is a minimum acceptable level of absurd required for you to change your mind on any decision; a tipping point when the no becomes a yes, or the yes becomes a no. It is extremely important to recognise that money is not the only motivator in an equation like this, and it certainly isn't the best.

Fear, anger, love and hatred in particular, but more broadly emotion in general, work in these equations. How scared, for example, do you have to be before you agree that all data needs monitoring by the state? How angry do you need to be before "Adolf Hitler's Nazism" seems like a reasonable solution to your problems? How much do you have to hate someone before you could stomach the state murdering them? What about a group of people? Could you think of any group of people- and be honest at least to yourself- that you wouldn't mind the state annihilating? Generally, when faced with this question people might be tempted to close themselves into the box of characteristics already persecuted throughout history- race and religion in particular- and as such find that question abhorrent. But what about paedophiles or rapists- could you not see yourself agreeing with society being rid of those groups? Truly? What about people who have tortured and raped children? If we could get that cohort of people together, would you not be at least placid, if not complicit in the state's decision to kill them? If not, can you honestly say that there is no possible scenario you would be? Perhaps, perhaps not. But be honest, and *think* about it.

We often see manipulation as a transaction, which it often is; but we fall short of understanding manipulation when we see it as merely a transaction, or one exclusively reserved to the exchange of tangible capital. Manipulation is so much more than that. It is a condition of being, a necessity. It is the ever-present clay tempting and tantalising would be sculptors with its universal potential. We also fall short of understanding manipulation if we believe that financial manipulation- using money to achieve a desired outcome that without the promise or utilisation of the monetary motivator would not have happened- is the most potent, most common or even the most useful form of manipulation.

That crown goes to one thing and one thing only, something explored in passing above and something we all have in abundance. As well as that, it is a resource passively exploitable outside the realms of our control: emotion. Emotion is the key to the door of ultimate manipulation, and is the reason why we are all, universally, susceptible to it. We often control our emotions as much as possible in regular daily life- at work, at home, out with friends- and shy away from being too emotionally overzealous. We can do this because we are aware of the stimuli that we are likely to face on any given day in any given place under certain circumstances (hence why we control them as much as possible; we are prepared by virtue of experience. This is also partly why children, naturally inexperienced as they are, struggle). We understand that we are likely to meet with conflict at work, or at the very least to meet with difficulty, and we understand the appropriate, professional, emotional responses to *most* of those difficulties. Within politics, as a population, we are generally much less educated, much less prepared and much more vulnerable to emotional volatility or reactionism.

The problems presented to us by politicians are unique, in so far as they are, firstly, only problems if presented in a problematic way, and the paradigm they are presented within is reciprocated by you (a "problem" for one can easily be an irrelevance or even a good thing for another; Brexit for example). The extent to which they are a problem is entirely at the discretion of the political commentator comprehending and explaining the problem, and the reaction by the listener- by you- is one ripe for the engineering: when it comes to political problems, we are often unequipped to decipher the nuances and intricacies of the issue with the same experienced vigilance as we are when dealing with other situational and emotional problems.

In the same vain, if a political party or an ideology can convince you that it is the *right* party or ideology, understood as *morally* right (a concept inextricably linked with emotion), then that party can convince you to support it, and by proxy, its agenda. That party can utilise your manipulable state for power, relevance and change. Your emotions are capital, and it is the concept of universal manipulability which allows for that capital to be harvested and transformed into power; it is your emotions most attacked by the manipulators that be, it is your emotions which render you susceptible to political allegiance and alignment. It is your emotions, the same emotions we all have in some capacity, which allow for politicians and political commentators to command your support (or to lose it), and it is our manipulable state which allows for this to be the case, a manipulable state overly exacerbated by underexposure, lacking understanding and lacking education on all the concepts and foundations feeding politics.

The capital this produces in the right (or wrong) hands is paramount. The ability to manipulate is one entirely dependent on whether you are the strong or the weak; when it comes to politics and political, philosophical and ideological understanding, the general public as a unit is the uninformed "weak", but we are so often touted as the strong. We are told that we have the "power" to enact change, that we have the "opportunity" to make the country and our lives better, that we have the "duty" to utilise our votes because they are our power, and with that power comes responsibility. It is not so clear whenever we are spun these rhetorical lines as to the precise nature of our "power"; less so the extent and reach of our "responsibility". In an ode to my opening point with this chapter-conclusive paragraph, we are all vulnerable to manipulation. All of us.

VII
Ideology and Morality.

"Any morality is nothing more than a mere system of valuations which are determined by the condition in which a given species lives"- Fredrich Nietzsche.

Ideology, engaging with the idea of universal manipulability, becomes an entirely different beast when rhetorical manipulation has been fully realised, and within a manipulating ideology one's mind has finally been captured; when the case has been made by politicians and you have concluded that the party they represent best reflects the ideology you most align with. Importantly, ideologies are not rigid or finite, but they are so often perceived as being, in no small part because it is incredibly difficult to reason someone away from a principle they have been conditioned into revering above all else when it has been tethered to an ideology. If someone has been convinced that an ideology is right- morally, philosophically, politically and socially *right*- then upon concluding this what they are in essence saying is that they have decided that the collection of ideas, problems and solutions highlighted and offered said ideology are the ones they think life should be conducted around. Ideology is an aggregate summation of how we think the world and human existence ought to be; It is incredibly difficult to alter that mindset in *most* people.

This is not to suggest, to reiterate, that ideology becomes finite after one assimilates oneself to its guidelines- just that your philosophy is given a name and becomes tangible and personal once an ideological moniker is embraced, similar to how a chicken becomes harder to kill once you give it a pet name. In gaining this personalisation, the thinker is tempted to relegate all philosophical autonomy to the doctrine of their chosen ideological persuasion, under the presumption that any questions which arise will henceforth be adequately answered by the newly established ideological home. This temptation (and the often succumbing to it) does not by any stretch mean or indicate that this ideological home will automatically provide any answers to your philosophical interrogations, let alone adequate ones, nor does it by any means signify that ideologies even possess the answers to them; more often than not, ideologies align with the pre-existing convictions of the individual, then shape them. They do not *provide them*. I call this the concept of a "Mydeology".

Mydeology and Ideology.

A "mydeology" or, more accurately, your "mydeology" is the exact and specific personal ideology that, were you able to completely and perfectly articulate all of your philosophical positions, moral convictions, political principles, social solutions and ethereal thoughts into a single written document, would be a manifesto for life, a guide to moral existence, according exclusively, precisely and uniquely to you as an individual. It is also worth noting that everyone's individual "mydeology" is completely unique; everyone's.

It is imperative to note that I do not reference one single ideology here[38], in the broad sense, but I reference "mydeologies" as the collective group of manifestos unique to each individual mind, understood as the document that would be created should each mind suppose to write one and be able to perfectly articulate every single thought they had concerning politics, philosophy and morality; an *individual* ideology as constructed by the individual's unique collection of experiences through life. For example, you may consider yourself a Tory just as Boris Johnson, or Rory Stewart, but your values of right and wrong, your morality, your actual, true, complete ideology- your mydeology- will be different from the two. Perhaps vastly different, perhaps not so much, but certainly in some identifiable way, different.

---

[38] The concept of a "mydeology" does not subscribe to any faction or avenue of thought specifically; it is a concept of its own accord, just as the concept of "ideology" concerns all ideologies and is entirely amoral in its own right. Categorisation can come later, but is not intrinsic to a mydeology.

Ideology is often erroneously confused as a developer (producer) of morality, in so far as it supposedly produces an idea of what is *morally* true and offers us an idea of what is right and wrong. This is not the case, because of a small nuance, and the distinction needs to be clear: Ideology does not develop morality in the thinker or subscriber; we have morals and morality without ideology. Instead, it **manufactures** morality within the thinker or subscriber. For it is not true that any one single ideology is objectively moral; nor is it accurate at all to suggest that any one ideology is objectively immoral. Morality is not static, and the ability to even have a discussion about morality is proof enough of this point to progress confidently[39].

But what, then, is morality? Are ideologies merely a collection of moral positions? Are morals a summary of multiple ideologies? What is the *relationship* between an ideology and morality? This relationship is a complex one. Morality is one of many factors which *attract* you towards an ideology. It is an aspect of your philosophy, and a component of your mydeology. Morality is perhaps the most individually important of these factors, as our morality has a more pronounced impact on all other facets of our ideological development. It is also along moral lines that our ideological allegiance tends to proliferate. Even if, for example, we consider ourselves market driven, we are rejecting some moral standards and applying others. This means that ideology is identified as an extension of our morality, and many of the ideological positions we align with are identified as morally just. The journey of moral realisation, having been assimilated with the ideology to which we align, then continues developing along *that* ideological rule book. We quite quickly go from rule maker to rule taker.

The relationship between ideology and morality is a complex one; both are inextricably linked; both are concepts which feed each other. At the core of it, ideology would probably be not just useless, but pointless as well, if it were not inextricably linked to morality; all worldly action would instead simply be expressions of pragmatism. How best to achieve the best iteration of human existence and co-operative living- this being in essence what ideology is- is at its very core *a question of morality*. Ideology offers sanctuary to a mind plagued by ethical static, ethical white noise, and this is why our ideological leaning is *always* fluid- because ethics and morality too, are *always* fluid, in the broadest

---

39 In so far as to be able to even discuss "right" and "wrong" in their moral context is to both acknowledge and accept that there are always different ways to quantify either, and that one's individual quantification depends entirely on them as a person, understood as the person they are being the total sum of all their experiences hitherto.

sense of their understanding. There are countless thought experiments available to illustrate this point, so I won't be so banal as to produce my own; the "trolley problem" as introduced by Phillipa Foot is an often cited and excellent example[40].

The most acute danger of this- one of the many dangers- is that once you have as an individual decided that your rules fit well with a certain ideological leaning, philosophical trend or individual ideology, you are often captured therein; ideology offers clarity to your thinking, and quickly becomes a *cause* in and of its own right[41]. Fluid though ideological leanings may be, the liquid is often thick and highly viscous; difficult to escape once you are in it; easy to drown in. The ideological trajectory- that is to say, the journey of how we arrive at our ideological identity- starts usually quite mainstream, with either Labour or the Tories (in the UK), somewhere left or right of centre, as a combination of prolonged exposure to these throughout our lives and the good intellectual practice of dipping your toe in the shallow end of the pool manifest themselves in centrism. It progresses and develops when you have finally had enough experience in life to at least show an *interest* in right or wrong (in the political, ideological and philosophical sense), and have some idea of what caused the problems you have faced over the course of your life, as well as what has offered the solutions of most efficacy to them.

From their initial ideological destination, the thinker, the ideological subscriber, the aforementioned ideological *rule maker*, can be tempted one of two ways- right or left- and is usually tempted further down the ideological rabbit hole they originally stumbled upon when first applying their rules. The right usually shifts right, the left *usually* shifts left. Occasionally you get a right to left shift, arguably more often but still seldom will you see a left to right switch.

Ideology often trumps mydeology in many ways, usurping your energy by offering it a tangible cause- power- and conflating. Mydeology is much more pure, and a much more accurate reflection of your moral composition than any ideology could ever be, but it is mired by many immutable characteristics. For a start, we are burdened by our own ignorance. Could it be that my opinion is

---

40 Philippa Foot, "*The Problem of Abortion and the Doctrine of the Double Effect*" in Virtues and Vices (Oxford: Basil Blackwell, 1978) (originally appeared in the Oxford Review, Number 5, 1967.)

41 A faction of thought as a cause is an idea that we have to wonder no distance to understand as a principle; take Marx and Marxism, for example, or socialism, or free market capitalism, or liberalism; ideology as a cause has always been and will always be a phenomenon prevalent in any society with any degree of free thought.

based in falsehood? Do the statistics support me? Are two positions I hold
intellectually compatible? What do I know about politics? A myriad of questions
can strike anyone seeking to establish some political standards and moral
positions, all questions which are answered if you relegate them to the political
party structure or the cult of an ideology. If you're a "liberal" in America, all the
arguing is done for you by a plethora of quite educated and learned,
professional minds. The same can be said for a "conservative". Secondly,
mydeology is impossible to discuss from a language perspective in daily life. If
we discuss, to stick with the example at hand, liberals or conservatives in daily
life, we have some broad knowledge of what we all mean. Sure, our definitions
might be somewhat different- sometimes in a nuanced way, sometimes in a
fatally disparate way- but we at least have that common ground of
understanding of language.

Ergo, ideology may well be fluid in principle, but fluidity leads to
inconsistency and a blurring of theory and practice. Again, for ideology to be a
useful concept it must be a mechanism towards affording change. Because of
this, ideology as defined by multiple minds to reference sets of congruent ideas
and moral positions always takes precedent in political practice, reality and
discussion over sporadic and perhaps seemingly incongruent positions
indigenous to one's personal mydeology. Once established, ideology thusly
tends to remain quite rigid, though demonstrably and theoretically fluid like
water in many ways.

Trans-idealism.

Our thoughts and principles, as guided by our experiences and
involvement with educators, parents and peers, will always, in some way, align
with an ideological position in accordance with any ideological spectrum. Just as
names are nouns, and we can identify what a verb is in language through
intrinsic definition, so too can we establish ideological positions from personal
principles. This is partly why it is a fallacy to suggest any moral or philosophical
position as "objective" or "apolitical". All rules of interaction are politics
incarnate, as politics is a discipline about the distribution and dispersal of power
coupled with their relationships with human interaction. When we do anything
with any other human we act politically to some degree. By definition, politics is
an unavoidable condition of interaction. Ergo, perhaps it is possible to say that
only the isolated individual, away from all other sentient life, is free from politics
and political interference; but then, such an individual would have no one to

interact with, no wider sentience to consider or navigate, and as such would not produce the circumstances which require humans to become political.

As such, whenever we choose to act a certain way in a certain scenario, whether that be consciously or unconsciously, we are exercising political decisions and aligning ourselves with a political ideology. All actions and all decisions are in some way political. The endeavour to produce a "political spectrum" of any kind has been an endeavour of quantifying these actions and now, because political spectrums exist and the foundations have been laid, these actions will be forever quantifiable, a valuable (and very historically recent) development, no doubt.

That isn't to say that actions are simple, or that quantification is easy. Kindness, for example, is a concept which may seem homogenous and straight forward at face value but is actually far from it. To be kind is not a simple or obvious operation, and how you choose to express kindness, along with how you understand it, is what kindness means specifically to you, in a mydeological sense. Your perceptions of what it means to be kind have been developed by your exposure to the word "kind", the explanation of its definition and examples of its application by your educators and peers. Is it kind to give your coat to a shivering stranger? Perhaps it is, and perhaps something like that would fall into most definitions of kindness.

But then, is it kind to tell a fat person they are fat? Or an ugly person that they are ugly? does the thought of doing it make you wince? Why? The answers to all of these questions likely indicate where you fit on the (or more precisely, "a") political spectrum. Your reasoning might be that there is no virtue in encouraging the fat person to continue wallowing in their fatness and as such, you have to highlight it to instigate change. Your reasoning might, on the other hand, be that telling a fat person they are fat is insensitive, and that insensitivity is never kind, that kindness is a good rule to live by and as such that there is no situation in which you should tell a fat person they are fat. The rules that govern your sensitivities here are rules directly governing your perceptions of appropriate human interaction: politics.

Of course, one's understanding and application of the concept of "kindness" doesn't and couldn't reveal your ideological affiliation by itself- and that isn't at all what this account is saying. But it *does* give a semblance of indication, a jigsaw piece, of the whole picture that is your ideological leaning. Kindness is perhaps a good example because it indicates a plethora of other things, such as one's sensibilities regarding tact, one's leaning towards individualism, the consideration one has for the consequences of their actions, whether one cares about the consequences of their words, amongst others. One's mydeology is formed by one's experiences and influences, one's ideology s a transition when our interpretations, experiences and influences are finally recognised as political, subjective and not universal. Our ideology is therefore a reflection of our mydeology, a secondary expression of preconceived rules by which we play the game of life.

This is in no small part due to the notion that we actively choose the ideology we think best reflects our own pre-concluded positions on morality, our values; our set of life rules. Our mydeology, however- our own unique set of experiences shared in their entirety by no other single individual being- is passive, and is what attracts us to an ideological home. The warmth we find when we get there, from the mydeological abyss of the metaethical cold through which we have journeyed, renders this newfound sanctuary, this ideology, a now insatiable, supra-permanent mental residence.

Usually, upon arrival at this new home, other questions will form and develop as we mature and the natural questions of life dictate that, with the new guidebook that is the ideology to which we have chosen to align, we enquire ever deeper about the rules we brought with us in the beginning, which seemed to best apply to life before, and seek clarification, expansion or elaboration of them whilst we are there. The further development of our rules by the ideological game we have chosen to play (the ideological leaning we have adopted) eventually renders our own rules all but useless, as the game itself so often becomes the rule maker whilst you are still gleefully rejoicing in play.

Once our minds are captured by an ideology and the individual mydeology which guided us to it is lost as a distinct, separate principle to that ideology; usually conflated with general morality. Over time- and not so much time for that matter- ideology becomes completely indistinguishable from morality. It ceases to be a home for morality to thrive and manifest itself in any individual or society whom so chooses to adopt it, and instead becomes inextricably linked to it. Even more sinister, morality becomes the diktat of the ideology, something to which subscribers of an ideology must, in order to keep their subscription, agree to or abide by almost unconditionally should they wish not to be banished. The transgender conundrum for the postmodern liberal sees this principle conveniently illustrated. It is the postmodern liberal diktat to accept anyone's self-identification as reasonable and, to a lesser degree, factual; to a more precise degree, actual.

That is to say, characteristic self-identification seems to be argued as the next logical step of progression from sexuality by the postmodern liberal in realising one's individuality and identity. It has been inextricably linked to the classical liberal tradition of free expression, which was hard won, and as such any opposition to it is denounced as bigotry, in this case the dreaded "transphobia"[42]. But you, as the learned and reasonable liberal mind that you are, do not accept that biology can be changed by something so whimsical as someone's emotion or mood. Sexuality is, you would assure the sceptic, based upon attraction and attraction is the *individuals* own business, but someone trying to tell you that black is white, that male *is* female, is something you just cannot abide, at least not without serious consideration. Unfortunately for you, the postmodern liberal does not care about your pathetic appeal to reason and has the power to revoke your liberal status until further notice. Hence, if you want to call yourself a liberal (which is an ideological position) you have to abide by liberal ideology.

Nowadays, if an ideology is agreeable (and aside from a select few positions) then you as the thinker are likely to change your thinking to suit it, instead of abandoning it altogether in favour of your pre-ideology mydeological convictions. This is a powerful reversal of precedent, and a transition that goes almost entirely unnoticed because, well, why would we notice this? It's an extremely complex (and for the most part irrelevant) line of thinking that would be completely untenable in most daily scenarios, and largely unproductive. Offering ideology so much consideration in every decision you make, or action you take, just isn't feasible. Which is why ideology seeps into our mentality and ethos, sneaks into or lives and consumes our actions peacefully, without need for any violence or force. Ideology develops because of our realisation that mydeological convictions are not actionable beyond the individual, and cooperation is the key to enacting change.

It is in ways like this that ideology can become a cult of its own right. When we forget that morality and moral direction guided us towards an ideological home (and why would we not, considering that we rarely actively consider this at all) we forget that we owe no allegiance to an ideology, and that we do not have to change with it, or at least that we do not have to automatically *accept* any changes ideologies enact, profess or dictate. Thusly, ideology *becomes* morality, when you have accepted it as your intellectual ethical home, agree that it is *the one strand of thinking* that has your best interests and deepest desires at its heart, and suppose that it is the only way to enact political manifestations of those interests and desires.

---

42 One of the many modern "phantom phobias" which seem to be created without a second thought for what a phobia actually *is, by definition.*

It is when ideology becomes morality that it penetrates not just your intellect- your mind- but also your emotions; your heart. Soon, ideology becomes a friend, and a universal justification for almost anything- that is to say, that almost every problem can be addressed, dealt with and justified through the lens of any ideology. There is not a single issue that cannot be addressed by any ideology at least in some part, save for the rare occasion your chosen ideology completely denies the existence of a particular issue (although, to deny the existence of something is still to acknowledge it, as a concept at least). Here, a transition occurs: the idea of ideology *manufacturing* morality, as opposed to *developing* morality, shifts again once your mind is truly snared by an ideology, and once that ideology has ratified and further manufactured within you a deeper moral code, it then has the ultimate ability to delegate morality according to its own doctrine, to change your thinking altogether. Your philosophical thoughts become ideological facts; this new morality becomes engrained.

This is where the conflation outlined at the beginning of this short chapter is born, and also why it is so subtle. It is here too, in the passive acceptance of anything and everything your chosen ideological home has to say, that the nefarious aspects of all ideologies, in the form of their manipulation qualities, are hidden, not least in their seeming and often easily justified reasonability. If your moral development has been thus far a foundation upon which an ideology could be built, then why would that ideology *not* seem reasonable? It's a fair and forgivable conclusion.

Virtue and virtuousness are the perfect disguise for ignorance and anger, for hatred and rage. If your ideology claims something as desirable, then your actions and emotions expressed in pursuit of that desirable thing are always veiled in virtue. Emotions such as ignorance and hatred may at first glance, and almost by definition, seem anti-moral in their nature, but they are an absolutely necessary part of the moral developmental process; for, if you cannot humanly feel things such as ignorance, anger hatred or rage, or worse still, can't identify them when they're presented to you, can you even truly claim to have any knowledge of their "desirable" diametric opposites? These "negative" emotions are critical in fact, for not only identifying what is desirable and undesirable- ultimately, what your goals should be- but also as a barometer for the importance of those things.

It is specifically within this principle- that these "negative" emotions are inevitable in life- that the power of ideology comes to its apex: once fully adopted, the ideology *directly controls* the stimulus for those negative emotions just as much as it controls the stimulus for any *positive* emotions. Positive and negative[43], as we ought to all be familiar, are often considered some of the founding principles of what we perceive as moral- positive being "good" and negative being "bad"- and the ideology to which we subscribe having ultimate power to control these reactions and perceptions dictates, by extension, that it also has the power to completely and totally shape our morality. Modern liberalism- or postmodern liberalism (PML, which we will discuss in much greater detail a little later on), as it much more accurately should be described- is a good illustration of this principle in action. As it develops its theoretical foundations, something it absolutely is doing in real time during the second decade of the twenty first century, we are seeing the morality of its disciples changing and altering, again in real time, in no small part because they fear the wrath or abandonment of the ideology (and as such their purpose) should they dissent, as outlined previously.

Take Justin Trudeau as an extraordinarily convenient and pertinent example of this: caught on camera in 2001 gleefully (and entirely innocently) blacking up his face for an Arabian nights themed fancy dress[44], he has since become a subscriber of the idea that so-called "blackface" is inherently and vehemently racist, something to inspire feelings of resentment and anger. He has become a subscriber of the postmodern liberal ideology and its doctrine, and has relegated all philosophical autonomy- which he clearly used to have- to the whims of postmodern liberalism. Trudeau's reaction has been an interesting one; he has apologised, saying that he "should have known better" *(ibid)* and that he sometimes gets too "enthusiastic" about costumes.

Really? He should have known better? Very clever, very political. How could he have possibly known better when what he did wasn't considered vexatious or wrong at the time? What it seems like he is saying there is that it actually wasn't a problem back in 2001, when postmodern liberalism hadn't engulfed us all in its tyrannical grasp. It wasn't a problem until PML introduced new age thought crime whilst conquering our language. It was not wrong in

---

43 The dichotomy- or continuum- of positive and negative has been the basis for or a factor in the development of many philosopher's theories of right and wrong, from Kant in "*The Groundwork of the Metaphysics of Morals*" to Ayn Rand in "*the Virtue of Selfishness*".

44 <https://time.com/5680868/justin-trudeau-brownface-photo-apology/>
Note as well that when he did it, he was a teacher, not a student; he was responsible and supposedly developed.

2001, when Trudeau still had the luxury of being able to think for himself, free of the political shackles of PML, and that he is merely paying lip service to the vocal minority who believe it became a problem. Unless, of course, what he is admitting is that he was a racist, that he meant it to be taken maliciously and that he should have only known better than to get it on camera; though, even the biggest cynic amongst us would have a hard time selling that line... So I will presume, with good faith, that he meant nothing malicious by it and was simply playing a character. Curious he felt the need to apologise if that's the case, and one can't help but wonder what his reaction to Donald Trump or an opposition Canadian politician being caught doing the same thing would have been.

The same can be said with the attitudes of postmodern liberals towards gender. Based around no hard science whatsoever, the debate surrounding gender has, particularly since circa 2014, become intolerably venomous and shrouded in this veil of the presumed virtue afforded to the postmodern liberal position of unilateral tolerance. Something that was previously relegated to the sparsely populated intellectual vaults of absolute fact- the notion that there *are* unquestionably only two genders, aside from some exceptionally rare anomalies- was something postmodern liberalism saw fit to completely challenge as an idea and in doing so completely (and arrogantly) conflate the ideas of gender and sexuality. It could to do this as an ideology because its disciples forfeited their individual autonomy surrounding the development and implementation of philosophy. We now find ourselves locked in a world where it is seen as acceptable, as dictated by postmodern liberalism which is the most ostensibly dominant ideological position in the west at the moment, for people to use this notion of "pronouns" and "transgenderism" as ammunition to define their virtuousness and assert their moral supremacy. Ideology transitioning into morality in real time, beyond- and this is crucial- the followers' previous moral positions. Ideology begins to take not just precedence, but to impose dominance as the group thinking intensifies and metastasises.

Morality and Learning.

Throughout life there is no *a priori* morality, there is no default, automatic moral position. You don't have to look very far to identify the truth behind that statement- gender dependent abortion in east and south Asian communities for example, the differing punishments for things like blasphemy across the globe, the treatment of homosexuals in the east vs the west. Simple and straight forward examples to identify this premise that morality comes before ideology, and that shared morality so often becomes collectivist ideology. The journey, however, perhaps contrary to the tone of this book thus far, is not necessarily one of strict indoctrination.

A child will hit until he is told that hitting is not the right thing to do; that hitting is *wrong.* As the child gets older, he may or may not be told, when his perceptions of reason and cognitive faculties have developed further, that hitting in *some* circumstances *is* the right thing to do. But what circumstances? Is it right to "punch a Nazi" as certain factions of the extreme left would suggest? What about to punch someone stealing a chocolate bar from a shop? Perhaps that chocolate bar is to feed their child, then what? The way you make these moral decisions and navigate these moral problems is to implement all the building blocks of your *mydeology* up to that point. Sometimes, you will be confronted with an issue that no previous experience has prepared you for and no external ideology guides you through; in these scenarios, you will have to laterally consider your "mydeological" convictions to determine the appropriate moral action.

Suppose, for example, you stumble upon a bag with £100,000 cash inside it. There is no one around, there are no cameras, and you can easily get away in mere seconds because your car is parked around the corner. For the sake of this argument, let's say you can be *certain* you won't be caught. What do you do? Keep it, acting in a purely expedient way? If not, why not? The answer to this question *absolutely* depends upon your moral convictions, and ideology is not separate to these. It is directly influenced by them, and actually usurps them for its own agenda.

Because of this developmental process, and because the attraction to whichever ideology you *choose* to align with is developed by the morality you have learned and throughout your life refined, the unique mydeology which you alone produced and to which you alone subscribe, we have a natural propensity to argue for and defend whatever ideology we have concluded as sovereign in our own minds. Following this, if we see something going against the sensibilities of the ideology to which we subscribe, we quite reasonably deduce it as "wrong". Naturally, when we see something as "wrong" we seek, almost as a reflex and always justifiably, to "right" it- or to at least highlight our concerns and illustrate why it is "wrong". The very fact that this back and forth, this intellectual conversation of moral valuation, can even happen, dictates that when we see something as "right" it is logically a frustration to us if others cannot see it; or even worse still, if others see our "right" as their "wrong".

Because the vast majority of the population are generally not heavily celebrated orators of philosophy, morality, ideology or politics, nor are we all natural conversationalists, we approach these issues with the assumption that because we are so obviously "right" and because our moral standing and deological subscriptions are based on reason, that to any *reasonable* person it ought to simply take exposure to our point of view to change their minds and help them see the light. Now, the more observant of you may very well raise the question "sure, we all think we are right but then, why doesn't the liberal listen to the Nazi, or vice versa? Why do we ignore people and differing opinions if we are aware of this principle, that exposure to *my* reasoning should be all it takes to convince someone of *my* thinking?". Well to you I would say good question, with a simple answer: we seldom, if ever, consider that *we might be wrong*, because when it comes to ideology and opinion, *we aren't.* Different moral positions can exist in parallel because the truth of things like political theory and morality is *entirely* subjective. This assertion is of critical and crucial importance to understand. If you read anything from this book it should be this paragraph- read it, re read it and understand and consider what it is saying.

There is a distinct difference between "truth" and "fact", one which the postmodernist has sought to monopolise in the 21st century but nevertheless a difference explainable and observable by all factions of thinking. All facts are true, but all truths are not factual. The easiest way to illustrate this without sinking into a philosophical quagmire is to argue the facts and truths of language. For it is factual, as a matter of semantic necessity, that all rapists are criminals, or that all bachelors are single; those statements are also true. However, jokes, for example, whilst reliant entirely on language and understanding similar to the statements offered before, are completely subjective. If a joke makes you laugh, you might say it is true that the joke is funny; if it doesn't, then you might say that it is true the joke is not funny. Neither statement would be factual, but both would be true.

"Wrongness" is often assumed by the population as some easily quantifiable concept, again entirely ignorant of phenomenological or metaethical enquiry, and similarly ignorant to the distinctions explored above. Wrongness is indeed easy to define and quantify at a subjective albeit truthful level, but at an objective, factual level, not so much. Opinions- which ideologies are *always* collections of- are never wrong. They may be *founded* in falsehood or misinformation, for example a hatred of a certain race or culture, but that doesn't mean the opinion, of itself, *is* wrong. It doesn't even mean that to base one's opinion upon misinformation is intrinsically wrong; indeed, that is a matter of opinion in itself, and whatever your opinions are on any of those things, they are components of your own *mydeology*. Does your mydeology accept the premise that ideology built upon misinformation is wrong, or does your mydeology simply just not care? If you think that to base one's opinion upon misinformation is wrong, why do you think that? Can we even suggest that anything is "misinformation" if we don't know *all the information* that it is possible to know? Certainly, in politics, it seems like there is always a counter point to even the most seemingly ironclad statistic, the most innocuous piece of information, or the most tenable position.

Holocaust denial, as ruled so recently in September 2019 as not being protected by article 10 of the European convention on human rights (ECHR)[45], is in essence the European Court of Human Rights asserting that there *can* be objective political facts- a pernicious assertion that should be met with trepidation to say the very least, even in the face of such an agreeable application of the law; who's "facts" are the real facts and, perhaps with even more sinister potential, who's are to be ignored? Speaking to this, we can never know the information that people have been exposed to which has ultimately shaped their mydeology, and we must never assume that the entirety of that mydeology is just ignorance- to do that, by definition, would be extremely bigoted, and more importantly, intellectually narrow.

However, we all do this to some degree. Not always maliciously or arrogantly, it must be said, precisely because we have all been exposed to different information. If someone has based an opinion on information you firmly disagree with, or even know to be false, then it's justified that your reaction to someone voicing that opinion isn't going to be particularly welcoming. If you hold a contrary opinion to theirs based on let's say easily accessible and extremely convincing information, then your superiority complex isn't just justified, its necessary. You *should* feel strongly about your opinions and political positions, you *should* feel strongly about that which has contributed to your mydeological position. Truth does exist, but truth is not finite, nor is it necessarily universal. Truth, especially in politics, is a matter of information exposure, and it is as unreasonable to presume that everyone has been exposed to all the information they ought to be exposed to in any given situation, as it is to convince yourself that you have. Truth is a learning process, never ending and malleable. Truth should never be confused with fact, and the two shouldn't be used interchangeably in politics as they so often and so carelessly are.

---

45 Article 10 is: "freedom of Expression". It is the article in EU law which protects the individual's right to freedom of expression. "This right shall include freedom to hold opinions and to receive and impart information and ideas without interference by public authority and regardless of frontiers".

Facts and Truth.

The above point ought not to be addressed with anger or contempt, or bewilderment or some blind rallying cry behind the integrity of facts; nor should it be used as a platform to proclaim the unavoidable existence of postmodernism, let alone try to argue for the usefulness of the postmodernist position. It should be used as a sobering point of intellectual urgency. It should be used to initiate a process of reflection and an interrogation of the phenomenology behind "truth" and "truthfulness", "facts" and "factuality". We ought to use the point- that truth is not universal, especially regarding morality and politics- as an opportunity to expand our minds and our thinking beyond the usual intellectual rails we are bound to. Facts as well are regularly used as a disguise for a subjective truth, as a mechanism to "prove" a position; we will be offered a fact in the hope that we accept it indicates some truth.

Facts are also often used, in politics at least, with disingenuous intentions. They are used because of the seeming authority they have by convention, in order to present dishonestly a point which might be fragile or intrinsically weak. The entire political spectrum does this, and the fetishism for fact based argument is an alarmingly self-destructive one; not least because politics, as discussed throughout this account, is the implementation of ideology which is the produce of philosophy, all of which is at its core based on heavy opinion established as truth, not objective fact (if such a thing can even exist in politics). What is "true" often depends entirely on your ideology and philosophy to begin with. Free market economics work, for example, only in accordance with your understanding of what ought to be achieved by an economic model and the proclivity of the free market to achieve it. The same can be said for social welfare; the fact that there are thousands of homeless people in Britain is of itself inconsequential; meaning has to be attached in some way.

When homelessness as a fact is used to infer some ideological "truth", perhaps that austerity has been the culprit or that capitalism has failed, that same fact is a bold and tactical appeal to emotion. Even still, other questions are not answered with it as a simple statement. So what if austerity made people homeless? What relevance does that assertion have to anything? There is a whole faction of thought dedicated to the idea that reduction of state expenditure is not just desirable, but magnanimous- how does the anti-austerity stance deal with these people? And regardless, surely it's a correlation, not causation? Either way, it's certainly not a matter of fact. This internal conversation speaks to the principle of intellectual dishonesty; that people will willingly make a point they know is easy and seemingly infallible, to control the discourse and present their position as more credible, tenable or useful than it is. This principle is something we can witness nowadays through the majesty of the technology which affords us a historically unparalleled window into the minds of millions of people on demand, technology in some cases which sees people engage in ideological skirmishes to argue such points.

There is a rarely discussed conflation of ideals hidden in these ideological skirmishes. For, as they materialise and become more and more intense, we forget (by virtue of the fact that most of us simply do not care) precisely where the positions we are arguing come from. Are they produce of our mydeological convictions, predating any ideological alignment? Are they matters of morality or merely political consideration? And precisely what is the distinction? Are they truly what you think or are they simply positions you have seen presented by people you revere or support? How precisely have you arrived at the position of argument you are holding, and why precisely do you steadfastly argue it?

Political, philosophical and ideological discussion rarely relies on "factuality", and even when it does, it often relies on it to make an intentionally irrefutable, dishonest point. The contributing factors to the positions we argue are much more regularly factors of (inherently fluid) truth; experiences, political exposure, life lessons etc- things which are a part of *your* mydeology, *your* individuality, more so than your ideological persuasion. Bespoke offerings of your own philosophy bolstered and reinforced by the agreement and refinement offered by your ideological alignment.

It is important we interrogate the ways in which our opinions come to the surface and are articulated, because often it is a journey we ignore altogether, like so many such journeys in life. If we suppose that we base our positions on facts, or even on truth understood as it has hitherto been discussed, we are still completely ignoring the crucially important questions of precisely what produced those facts or truths in the first place, and whether they are indeed "factual" or "truthful" at all. As Hayek suggested around the middle of the 20th century, that the academic branches of history and the social sciences were dominated by left leaning dogmatic positions, so too would that same observation be a prudent one today. Ignoring for a moment the quagmire of discussion that is the ideological bias of western academia, and the devastating effect that is having on western thinking and discourse, suppose such an observation were factual, for a moment. Suppose we all agreed this to be the case (understanding that I understand we probably don't). But suppose we do. Can't we see the sheer chasm of intellectual bias that this ideological domination might drag us into? And as such, isn't it worth seriously and igorously considering, and questioning with equal vigour? The same can, of course, be said for all implicit bias, but the point is that so rarely is this consideration given, and opinions are supposed as manifestations of truth with zero consideration offered as to what it means to be a "manifestation of truth".

Politicians seize this idea of implicit truth. They thrive on it, because it can be used as a foundation upon which to construct a narrative and build an argument, which can then be parroted by multidimensional followings; those who initially believed the truth, those who believe the narrative, those who believe the argument or those who simply believe the politician. Outside of strict academia (and even there more often than not) ideologies are shaped by a plethora of factors and the inconsistency of these factors is useful for anyone looking to weaponise ideology for the purpose of acquiring power.

An interesting factor in these mailable truths is that we arrive at the truths which we reason as right to us, and look for those arguing the same positions as solidifying voices of authority. Politically speaking this is an incredibly valuable human proclivity, as it allows for the identification of not just a message, but a ready-made audience prepared to receive a would-be politicians message and proliferate its exposure, as they try to sell it on the politician's behalf.

By virtue of this- the fact that what you think is right *is right to you*, and that what is right to you is logically universally applicable- the ideology to which you subscribe produces within you an obligation to be expressed. We as individuals tend to want the best-case scenario to happen, and *generally* the best-case scenario for us, as individuals, can translate to the best-case scenario for society, as a whole, should it be adequately and properly scaled. Altruism for example, is a brilliant position here to which we can contrast broad individualism: altruism is right to the altruist, whereas the individualist will reason and justify that each individual looking after their own interests will inevitably produce the most fair and ultimately desirable society. The two seem diametrically opposed, and yet their desired results are broadly the same.

Conclusively, the point that should be drawn from this interrogation is as follows: we have the right to argue and present our ideology in open discussion, as many people indeed so do, but we *do not* have the right to have our opinions or our ignorance's *respected*. This conflation is often one of presuming people should respect truth as much as they respect fact, and that we have made no mistakes ourselves in establishing which is which. Whilst this is the conclusive point to consider, it is also the conclusive point that is almost always, ironically, ignored by the vast majority of people, mostly due to them counterintuitively accepting the logic and reasoning of rejecting ignorance where ever they find it, whilst simultaneously rejecting the idea that they can or do exhibit any. Because of the above factors discussed hitherto, we often feel like there is a righteousness to our opinions, which gives them this moral superiority precisely because our opinions are the articulation of our mydeology, which is the manifestation of every and all of our earthly experiences both physical and spiritual, aligned with an ideology. Its value, that of our morality and the ideological positions our morality encourages us to and even dictates that we should arrive at, is derived from its time served nature and is therefore, always relevant.

Our ideology is a representation of that which we hold intellectually dear enough to live and die by, that which our philosophical journey of self-realisation has guided us towards. The emotional, intellectual and enlightened expression of all our experiences, opinions, difficulties and character traits. It takes some time to become an "ideology" per se, and it remains fluid for much of the process of its development. This fluidity is good for political parties, because it gives them all a chance to make their sales pitch, to make their case for your support. It is at this point that ideology perhaps becomes the most dangerous.

VIII
Weaponising ideology.

"In order to achieve their ends the planners must create power... of a magnitude never before known. Their success will depend on the extent to which they achieve such power. Democracy is an obstacle to this suppression of freedom."- Fredrich Hayek.

***

For political power as a concept (and for it to be a useful, achievable goal) ideology is the most important thing bar none, especially in a western liberal democracy. Ideology is what gives credence to the would-be politician's message, direction to their policy and attractiveness to their party- it is the commodity that needs utilising should a political party wish to be successful at all the things a political party ought to be successful at. Engaging with the developments of ideology discussed throughout this book, some critical considerations must be embraced should a party wish to do this. We must also constantly keep in mind this fact: political parties, by necessity, seek to utilise ideology in some capacity to achieve power.

The journey of ideology is a curious one, and to properly interrogate it, we must establish where we start from, and where we end up. People *en masse* often labour under the misapprehension that thoughts only become ideology when they are seized by someone seeking power or claiming authority, and used to further an agenda; that their thoughts, moral positions and political opinions are somehow "non-ideological" until someone, some pseudo academic or opportunist politician, supposes to quantify them under an ideological umbrella. The idea that believing in redistributing wealth because you're a "good person" somehow removes its ideologically socialist connotation until someone chooses to create an ideology called "socialism" and adopt that premise. It does not.

Ideology is not the creation of humanity, like mathematics was not the creation of humanity. Ideology is just how we express these concepts and ideals in a digestible, logical, quantifiable way, just as mathematics is used to express a vast multitude of understandings and expressions. Redistribution is to socialism as 2+2 is to 4. It is an expression of aggregate knowledge and refined understanding, not an expression of a whimsical ideologue looking to create a cause, but an expression of political action which, just as mathematical equations were used to create the nuclear bomb, can be utilised for a powerful agenda under the banner of the ideology in question. This, partly, is the reason why ideologies are so often so fluid, with many accepted iterations all falling under the same umbrella, and also why we need a scale along which to measure and quantify ideologies. Over the years there have been many iterations of this, from the linear "Communist left to Fascist Right" model, to the horseshoe model demonstrating ideological similarity at the extremes, to the oft cited and now infamous "political compass"[46].

What is Ideology?

Political actions can never be ambivalent. They can never be unideological, because they always- always- align with a position on any ideological scale. They have to be quantifiable, we need a way of developing and refining our ideological understanding in the same vain as extremely meticulous and logical disciplines, like mathematics to continue with the same analogy, need developing and refining to ratify meaning and test theory. Philosophy and thought need structure. Everything to a certain extent needs structure. Let us for a moment consider that the increasingly offered idea of "forgetting all political allegiance and silly ideological namesakes and just doing

---

46 Available at: <https://www.politicalcompass.org/>. It is a dual axis test which separates economic and social positions to create an assessment of ideological position with more dimension. Many modern models of the ideological spectrum have adopted a multi axis model.

things for the betterment of humankind, regardless of politics" is a noble cause, and that we want to play it out.

It may very well seem straight forward at face value; simply do things to improve peoples' lives and ignore the factional, political or ideological elements of those actions. Just get them done. Okay... But what does it mean to "better someone's life"? What is it that comes to mind when you think about "improving" people's lives? Do we come full circle, and use ensuring people have the basic necessities (food, water, shelter, sex) as our yard stick? Surely we would all agree that to go back to such a basic point would be regressive, not progressive? If so, then maybe we ought to come to a modern understanding: what's say we make everyone rich? A good Idea, right? Perhaps, but then how do we do it? How rich precisely do we make everyone and more importantly, what defines rich? Avoiding getting lost in a quagmire of rhetorical questions, the above hopefully demonstrates the crucial Achilles tendon of the myth that things can be achieved apolitically: that negotiation is always necessary, and disagreements happen. If philosophy is the process of thinking and consideration, then politics is their enactment; Ideology is the flavour.

Decisions all command broadly speaking political solutions, no matter how large or small, because you always have to preclude some option or options in order to choose another. In that regard, politics could I suppose be described in its broadest sense as the art of making decisions. Politics is also the art of making judgements, and those judgements are always quantifiable as ideological. Decisions based on judgements are always political, and always have an ideological slant. This is why we cannot preclude ideology from the conversation; this is why we cannot solve any problems without ideological involvement, particularly problems relating to large groups of people describable as 'communities' or 'societies'; those problems are always political as a matter of fact, and ideology is always an important element of the ensuing discussion.

The qualification of "ideological" has come through the development of our understanding of the ideas we put into practice, not through the underhanded manufacturing of ideological "teams" with the ultimate goal of winning some game for power. This is not to say, however, that this does not happen: it certainly does, most notably in the form of the political party, but it must be understood and embraced that politics came long before the political party, that ideology is a quantification of our understanding of all political developments, and that politics happens at every level of interaction.

Postmodern Liberalism and Power.

The direction of this small chapter could have gone many ways, but I specifically chose this one because of its immediate relevance to *all* of our lives, at least in the west. This chapter will proceed with a further interrogation of that often referenced but seldom described ideological idol of the western hemisphere: liberalism. More specifically, the liberalism we have ended up with in the post-Thatcherite-Blairite caustic solution that is the prevailing ideology the west has been forced to endure for the last 35 years or so. Henceforth (and on many occasions, hitherto), we shall call this brand of liberalism "Postmodern liberalism", or PML.

PML, famously or infamously, began with Thatcher and Reagan. There was a shift in the late 1970s in the west, towards both free market economics and the overhauling of the role and size of the state (to cut a very long story unflatteringly short[47]). This shift was probably innocent enough- in so far as it did not have the intention of ushering in PML as we now know it- and Thatcher indeed succeeded at reducing the size, and re-defining the role, of the state; rolling back the frontiers of the state, as she called it. She shattered the post war consensus once and for all, sold off government owned houses, cut government services (aside from the police and armed forces), infamously collided with trade unions and championed private ownership, enterprise and business. Her heart was probably in the right place- as initially it probably was with Europe and joining the EEC- but quite quickly the monster of her legacy was free to metastasise; she had ushered in a new era of free market, globalist, small state consensus politics.

Far from producing an era of ideological conflict and constant political friction, the political brand ushered in by Thatcher was quickly embraced by her successor John Major, and usurped by none other than Labours fresh faced third-way pioneers Tony Blair and Neil Kinnock. Unlike the openly Keynesian, trade union and worker supporting socialist faction of mainstream politics that

---

[47] To interrogate this further, the likes of Francis Fukuyama (End of History and the Last Man), Noam Chomsky (Imperial Ambitions and Profit over Power) and Foucault (because of his interrogations of the development and dissipation of power in Discipline and Punish specifically) are a good start, though there are any number of social commentators and political theorists commenting around this transition.

abour had positioned itself as being in its first few years in opposition[48], and continued practising in sporadic stints in government, Neil Kinnock began a process of transformation, the completion of which was marked by the ascension of Tony Blair to power. This transformation, perhaps most infamously personified with the revision of Labours constitutional clause IV[49], saw New Labour embrace the free market, introduce tuition fees and broadly monetise education, support and maintain private involvement in state affairs- even expanding it with things like the infamous (and abysmally unsuccessful) Public Finance Initiative (PFI) schemes- and do little to reverse the state owned property sell off. New Labour enshrined PML, particularly economic policy, into cross-platform-British-political canon law. Blair embraced and won over the media with his "character" and "charm" (don't laugh), as well as in no small part his acceptance of the globalist free market status quo. Blair fortified the Thatcherite consensus across and beyond party lines, and this was spun as "Blairism".

Blair wasn't for leaving it to the history books- much less historians- to talk of, quantify and qualify Blairism. He wanted to carve a legacy all his own, and his secret weapon was genius: the welfare state. Or, in other words, to seek as a matter of ideological policy the increase of reliance- even dependency- of the individual on the state. It is no surprise that postmodern liberalism liked its Thatcherite, neoliberal foundations, of reducing the financial burden and reliance of the individual on the state, because in no small part of how much it averted the gaze of public scrutiny from its general direction. Encourage people to concern themselves with themselves and they will hopefully not concern themselves with the government and the state. But the problem was, naturally, the lack of *control* that came with this as an ideological agenda. Encouraging in the individual increasing personal responsibility and autonomy is a road at the extreme end of which there is no state, no bureaucracy, and no establishment. Not anarchism, per se, but close- perhaps the libertarian vision of an ideal society. This is bad for anyone in a position of power, especially anyone looking to increase or retain it. Blair recognised precisely this point, and inevitably had to change it, but he and New Labour nevertheless *liked* the fundamentals laid out by Maggie.

---

48 "Old Labour", from its inception to its demise.

49   Which   can   be   explored   in   their   glory   here: https://www.theguardian.com/politics/2015/aug/09/clause-iv-of-labour-party-constitution-what-is-all-the-fuss-about-reinstating-it

The welfare state was his trump card. I was a child throughout Blairs tenure. In 1997, I was five years old. By the time he left, I was still just in high school. As described in earlier chapters, I was young and quite naive. That didn't, however, stop my inquisitive mind noticing things: building was the big one, of schools, houses, hospitals and fire stations, and most importantly to the younger me, play parks. There was a vast amount of building, and plenty of parks were included in this; they had all these modern climbing frames and play equipment. It was wonderful. And would you believe I had Mr. Blair and his cabinet to thank for that. As I got a little older and parks became much less of an immediate concern to me, I realised, cutting through this silver lined fog of infrastructure euphoria, just how much people were becoming *reliant* on the state.

Things like benefits, student finance and subsidised public transport were huge issues of the time. Any situation in which there was access to state money. We heard about benefit fraud, asylum seekers claiming billions from the state, abuses of the system and the rest. Plenty of it was hyperbole, and the real shame of it all was that within many of those narratives, the point was lost. Anger and disdain for these political straw men blinded people to the more difficult to digest (and difficult to articulate) notion that the state was moving to shackle them, long term. The more people there are reliant on the state, the more power the state has over *everyone*. Blair and his administration captured this principle excellently, across all walks of life, but perhaps education is the best example.

In monetising education, as Blair and his administration did in many ways but most overtly by introducing tuition fees to higher education, there was a false positive created: it looked like Blair was being extremely neoliberal in so far as he was shifting the onus of responsibility from the state to the private individual. Suddenly, we now had to pay for our own success in life; how very Thatcherite. Or so at least it seemed. Upon closer inspection, we see that it was actually a masterstroke of genius by a collectivist statist trapped in a developing neoliberal dogma. For you see the way in which students pay for their university lifestyle was by taking out a loan, which was essentially backed by who? You guessed it, the state. It was a ruse of privatisation and individualism, but it was brilliant- it locked a generation of students into a cycle of debt, which was essentially payable to the state. The state owned them. No wonder the incentivisation of bums on seats came shortly after. The numbers games played by Blair in education were the genius of his operation and his contribution to how postmodern liberalism developed. He demonstrated with skill how the control of the individual could be achieved from behind the smokescreen of ostensible individualism which had been championed by PML and successfully implemented into the British political, western liberal democratic ethos.

Controlling people is more than overt state coercion, and the modern PML state understands precisely this because of Blair and his contribution to the ideology. Locking people into a system of indebtedness to the state means not only do they owe the state hard currency, but that they also feel an obligation to thank the state for their successes, because of the obvious role in them the state has. This translates far beyond education too. Working tax credits, unemployment benefits, child benefits- many avenues of state subsidy- can create this reception, this doublethink, whereby people simultaneously believe in their freedom of choice but also hold the necessity of state intervention as sacrosanct.

When the state has the power, the state also shoulders the burden of both the individual's success and their failures. If one could somehow assimilate these successes to the state more so than the failures, one could lock people into a cycle of state reliance and desensitise them to the tyrannical governments such a system could usher in. In a world where state interference is good and conducive to the individual's success in life, even at the smallest level, then increasing state reliance can become a rallying recruitment drive for support by governments. Not only that, but any system "giving" people something that they need or want becomes, as a system, indispensable to those people. They are essentially bought and paid for.

Of all the ideologies in all the world to do this, PML has been the most sublime. Developed by the new right and galvanised by the new left, PML thinking has drowned political ideology in an inescapable conformity. Political parties have found that a reliant population is a docile population, and a docile population is a population from whom all the individual power can be extracted by the collectivist state.

New Labour, Old Tricks.

The genius of Blair and New Labour was to distinguish themselves markedly enough from the Tory party but not too much from the agreeable ideological status quo the Tory party had shepherded in, and was done in one specific way: they solidified the centre-ground, building upon its Thatcherite foundations and steel re-enforcing it with hollow, pseudo socialist desirability. Under New Labour, people weren't just reliant on the state; they were believers in it. The biggest problem presented by this ideology was the question of: precisely what was to happen to the none believers? Blair couldn't silence them, but luckily for him almost no one saw the potential for what has materialised, and they generally concerned themselves with real time critique, addressing the symptoms of the illness plaguing society, not the cause.

With the whole benefits cheat dialogue, for example, there was a huge paradigm shift in accepted modern lexicon and the semantics of political discourse, a huge shift in what you can say and how you can say it. This shift is easiest described as the transmutation of the "Weak/ strong continuum" into that of the "good/ bad continuum" instead. To describe someone or something as "weak" became tantamount to describing something or someone as "good", as bastardised as that transition is. Fighting for the weak became "fighting for the good", and of course, everyone wants to fight for good, right? The genius of the transition, as politically savvy as it was, indeed continued long after Blair. But how did this happen, and what does it mean? Well, that is probably best explained and demonstrated with an example, and perhaps an anecdote or two.

Even as recently as the '90s and the early 2000s, what constituted a strength and what constituted a weakness were often extremely easy to distinguish and transparently clear cut. To be physically strong, for example, was a "strength". Being tall, in good health, intelligent, wealthy, pretty or beautiful, were (are) all "strengths". Naturally, the more of these strengths in one's possession, the easier life would be - or at least, the better equipped one would be to deal with the regular plights and challenges of life. Unsurprisingly (and again, as recently as within this time period, quite obviously) the fewer of these strengths in one's possession (and the above list isn't an exhaustive one, I think it's fair to suggest that we can all add probably hundreds more to it), the harder their time on this good Earth was likely to be. That assertion could even go one step further; not only could someone *not possess* any of these strengths, but they could in fact possess some characteristic *weaknesses*.

Weaknesses like being short, fat, ugly, mentally ill, homosexual, being physically weak, being poor or any number of weaknesses that, again, if you remove any arbitrary and overly pedantic cynicism, almost anyone could coherently quantify. Weaknesses, the more of which you as an individual have, the more difficult your journey through life is destined to be. Quite obviously too, if again, we remove these notions of our postmodern liberal sensibility and our inclination now to act so sycophantically towards the PML mentality. Interestingly, at least one of these weaknesses, in some iteration or in some way, applies to almost everyone. In fact, they apply to the vast majority; even the wealthiest men on the planet are short, lacking in physical strength, physically unattractive or frail. These weaknesses apply to the vast majority of people, probably everyone. We all have some area of weakness.

What does this mean, for the PML narrative? It means that there is a vast cache of capital- political capital- available to anyone or anything so inclined as to capture and utilise this idea, this vast pool, of weakness. How does the budding PML thinker go about doing that? They make weakness desirable; turn "weakness" into "strength". Turn the very *idea of weakness* into the idea of strength. Even better, turn the idea of weakness into a strength *dependent* on collective co-operation. The new strength. Tell people that whatever it is you are selling can commandeer their weaknesses (which are still weaknesses, we just hate identifying them as such nowadays) and turn them, using the power of imagination and post truth magic[50], into their diametric opposites, into characteristics of strength.

Now, there are a few problems with this transition. You can't simply do this by bluntly telling people black is white and hot is cold. At least not that brazenly (though if you could it would have saved PML decades of hard labour). PML does however do it in a way that is akin to that brazen sleight of hand. Let us explore its methods sequentially, so as not to lose the message in the words.

The first problem is the problem of precisely how to turn a strength into a weakness. To do this, you have to for a second forget about the idea of weak and strong and instead focus your gaze on a concept which is much broader and easier to appropriate (or misuse). A larger, more forgiving foundation upon which to build an ideology, considering (as we should still be doing) that they are built exclusively around philosophy and morality: the concept of good and bad. 'Good and bad' is by absolutely no means as clear cut as 'strong and weak', and therein lies the brilliance. Being strong can be argued or categorised as generally a "good thing" and being weak can be seen as generally a "bad thing", but that is not a definition to be taken for granted, and it is not by necessity the automatic or objective default position; just, for the moment, more of a correlation we ought to keep in mind.

Another problem for postmodern liberalism is that 'strong and weak' are easier to quantify philosophically than 'good and bad', and it is within this problem where the acute interest of the PML thinker is peaked: a strength is anything that gives you a competitive advantage over someone else who does not have that thing, whether it be a characteristic, a mentality, an item or the serendipity of existing within a certain set of circumstances. A weakness, conversely, is any of the above that gives you a competitive disadvantage- whether that be by something you have, like ill health or a small physical

---

[50] A useful and indeed oft used tool and weapon in the arsenal of the postmodern liberal.

stature- or something you don't have, like money, a large house, political power or good looks. The dichotomy of "strength and weakness" is an easy dichotomy to identify, and both qualities are easy to characterise.

This characterisation is the basis of the precise problem facing the postmodern liberal, the characterisation that traditionally strength has often been broadly and axiomatically presumed as good and weakness has been axiomatically presumed as bad. It is good to be physically strong, intelligent, powerful or rich. It is bad to be physically weak, stupid, powerless or poor. If you keep the 'strong/ weak' dichotomy synonymised with the 'good/ bad' dichotomy, as it was largely throughout most of human history, then that capital of weakness we discussed just a moment ago becomes an opportunity lost for the would be thinker- the Post-Modem Liberal, in this case- seeking to use it as a mechanism to monopolise political power and proliferate the state.

The Proliferation of Power.

Power has throughout most of human history been the unique reserve of those exhibiting many of these aforementioned strengths, or at least, those most potently exhibiting the most useful strengths of any given group. "Strengths" were not and are not delegated on any sort of "fair" basis at all, and consequently they produce a natural hierarchy, a social hierarchy, a traditional hierarchy; whichever way you want to look at it, a hierarchy, very clear cut with the strongest at the top and the weakest, defined by these traditionally simplistic measures of strong and weak, at the bottom.

In the pursuit of fairness, a crusade headed by one word in the west and one word only (liberalism), seeing the few strongest at the top and the many weakest at the bottom has been thusly defined as the apex of unfairness. Postmodern liberalism has therefore found itself engineering its core narrative against the very quality of strength to be rare and valuable, and weakness to be abundant and undesirable[51]. This is how ideology and narratives are weaponised; this journey is perfectly exemplified by PML in its pursuit of power, in how PML renders strength as weakness and weakness as strength. Both qualities are stripped of their philosophical components and rebuilt into a mechanism of power. Ideology is fickle, because ideology is inherently

---

[51] An observation which could be lost in its unassuming single sentence guise but an observation of prevailing importance to this account.

dependent upon interpretation not just of the intention of that ideology by prospective followers, but its specific understanding of the words and concepts it uses to present that intention as an achievable goal.

PML utilises strength and weakness in this way, as it maintains the desirability of one but transfers it to the meaning of the other. PML relies on the desirability of the concept of "strength" and the useful ubiquity of "weakness". It flips their definitions, and in flipping their definitions completely upside down maintains the easy to register "good and bad" status quo of the dichotomy. PML has spent the last 40 years, since the ascension of Margaret Thatcher and Thatcherism, through the plight of Major, Blair, Brown Cameron and May, defining itself to transition this narrative, progressively latching on to the most pronounced "strong/ weak" dynamics it could until people accepted its own message and desired outcome. The culmination of this has been things like masculinity (strong) being described as toxic (weak) and anyone, particularly men, exhibiting femininity (weak) being celebrated as emotionally in touch (strong). Things like people being born male (strong) changing their gender to female (weak) because they were mentally enlightened enough to realise that they were born in the wrong body and refuse to remain oppressed (strong).

The "strong /weak" paradigm being transitioned in to the "good /bad" paradigm, and the subsequent ability of PML to posit that which used to be strong and good as transformed into being weak and bad has been the genius of PML and is a sinister testament to its archiatects. In doing it, PML has presented itself as the *de facto* position of the majority, in any and all scenarios, considering that the majority is *always* weaker than the minority[52], although PML would love to have you believe otherwise, owed in no small part to the fact that strength in any form is a rare character trait or biological gift; it is the exception, not the norm. In shifting the societal order to that of reverence for the weak, and in shifting the most desirable emotional capital from strength and victory to weakness and hollow virtue, the PML has created, in theory, a positive feedback loop of support. If more people will always be weak than strong, PML will always have more followers than dissenters; the observable benefit of this principle should be obvious and paramount.

---

[52] Not to suggest that the majority of any given demographic or population shares the *same weakness*, but more that in any given sample of individuals there will be a quantifiable hierarchy which resembles a pyramid; the narrowest point will house the strongest, the widest point the weakest. Those strengths and weakness do not have to be the exact same thing- for example sexuality- but will *always* be categorised with others sharing that *level* of weakness.

This is interesting in so far as postmodern liberalism did not just, as an ideology, wake up one morning and think to itself: "I am going to challenge societal hierarchy and posit my own". How, then, did this come to be? How does one presume to challenge the entire foundations of a society? How does one convince the masses of your message? The answer to these questions, over-simply put, is "sequentially". PML already had a huge pool of core believers (the weak) and a universal message of unity (bring the weak together in numbers and they will become the strong). Remember, PML looks to convince the world that the weak are more *valuable* than the strong; that they should be catered for and looked after above the strong; that strength is something to be dissipated or repressed, not celebrated or exploited, and certainly not for personal gain. This is something western mentality has practiced for hundreds if not thousands of years anyway; do you give up your seat on the bus for an elderly lady or a disabled person? Most of us probably do, or at least would do. PML has not had a tough job of convincing us of its virtues, it just had to bide its time, and increase its potency both steadily and gradually so as not to spook the population or make any mistakes afforded by overzealous policy.

Without getting lost in the development of postmodern liberalism- an issue I assure you deserving of a book all its own, and in any case one argued vehemently, articulately and extraordinarily competently by Nietzsche (and others) on numerous occasions[53]- the weaponisation of it as an ideology is visible in how postmodern liberals manipulate its position and its subsequent attraction to the masses, and this highlights the ultimate goal of ideology, as well as providing further insight into how ideology can be weaponised: as soon as an ideology can be seen as a road to power, it becomes a commodity; as a commodity, it has exponential value, well beyond that of simple moral virtue.

Using a commodity is an expensive practice, in no small part because commodities are finite. Ideologies have to demonstrate their value, they have to create usefulness beyond their initial conception and beyond their initial populism or appeal to the motivations of those seeking power. If an ideology relies too heavily on straightforward and explicit appeal, it will abruptly exhaust its value, and forever be nothing more than a fad. If an ideology is too superficial, it will abruptly exhaust its appeal. Ideologies need both an abundance of value and an abundance of appeal if they are to be successful in attaining the ultimate goal of all ideologies: full implementation. Implementation, for the ideology, is power. Power for an ideology is usefulness,

---

[53] In both *"Beyond Good and Evil"* and *"the Genealogy of Morals"* throughout.

and an ideology can only ever survive if it is useful in some way; if it serves a purpose.

IX
The Power of Ignorance.

"On their economic platform the BNP and Green Party are not dissimilar: both would object to a typical London restaurant, the Greens for the distance the food on the plate had taken to travel, the BNP for the distance the person serving it had." - Ed West

***

In the early 2000s, after a ten-year non-disclosure clause that was part of a settlement to a legal case heard in 1992-93[54] was all spent up, our televisions were suddenly graced by a trickle of adverts talking some spooky legal jargon about something called "PPI". This spooky jargon was received with a tepid bemusement, to begin with, whilst people weighed up the plausibility of anything that sounds too good to be true *actually* being true. Luckily for Britain, this was the one time that history was on the side of the dreamer, and a legitimate way of claiming back potentially thousands of pounds per customer- and millions of pounds per bank- was actually here. Why was it here? Because of so many things, not least the power of greed... But mostly it was here for one reason alone: the unrelenting power of ignorance.

---

[54] Available here for any inquisitive mind so inclined to have a retrospective look at what started it all. https://webarchive.nationalarchives.gov.uk/20140402182951/http://oft.gov.uk/shared_oft/super-complaints/oft825.pdf

You see, banks were so bold and arrogant as to literally steal billions (BILLIONS) of pounds from people who were looking to secure much needed loans, and they exploited their status as kingmaker in the lending equation that was pivotal to these average folks' lives. People didn't (and even still, don't) read the fine print, didn't even question this "PPI" which was appearing on their loan agreements because of one reason and one reason alone: the pure bliss of ignorance. Okay, maybe there wasn't *one* reason, and maybe it wasn't so poetically black and white as an idiom as old as time itself, but all of the reasons for accepting PPI- or at least all of the reasons for not questioning it- have ignorance at their heart.

Importantly to me as your humble author and hopefully to you as the valiant and gracious reader, as well as providing almost everyone over the age of 30 with a cheeky thousand-pound claim, this noughties endeavour of elite corruption managed to put a number on ignorance and present to us a foundation upon which to build a chamber of interrogative thought: £50 Billion[55]. An approximation of the collective sum of all that was owed by all the banks, or in other words, all that was stolen from the public. Herein, we see the tangible, monetary value of ignorance, and are exposed to the power one can harness from it. In the case of PPI, monetary profit and capital. There is no doubt that, regardless of what the banks will have to pay back, they will have made probably tenfold or more on the money they loaned out backed by their PPI capital. Even if they are made to pay back every penny of the £50bn, they will still have made millions or billions of pounds more. Quite clever really, and an alarmingly raw window into the ruthlessness and blurred morality of the modern financial world.

At this point, you might be asking the questions of what does all this have to do with politics and power? What revenue could such a fraudulent principle as PPI generate in the case of ideology? Well, amongst other things, profoundly dangerous levels of control, heightened manipulation and ultimately, Orwellian tyranny. For you see, convincing people of *truth* is one thing, but convincing people of *want* is another. People *wanted* these loans and were lulled into a state of ignorance in their pursuit. To generate a desire for what you promise you can deliver, to generate the marketer's demand to the businessman's supply, is to unlock the potential of an ideology in earnest.

---

[55] A figure contested, and intrinsically difficult to arrive at, but nevertheless available here: <https://www.thisismoney.co.uk/money/markets/article-7636407/As-mis-selling-scandal-wipes-profits-Lloyds-PPI-claims-costs-banks-76m-day.html>

Marxism would be meaningless if there wasn't a desire for the ideology. You are marketing, when it comes to ideology, just as much as when it came to cigarettes in the '40s and '50s, and many of the same tactics, rules and nuances apply. Most of these are overt and mundane, but the most dangerous, the most villainous, the most profoundly nefarious, are the subtle, passive tactics that prey on the target audience's susceptibility to manipulation, and their ignorance to the existence of that susceptibility.

In terms of ideology, these tactics are cleverly harnessed in national and international discourse, to conveniently narrow complex ideological "fine print" as it were- the metaphysical, ontological, semantic, metaethical intricacies and implications of ideologies- into easily digestible and understandable, overly simplified ideological concepts. The narrowing of all discourse in the USA into one of "conservative" versus "liberal" is a good example of this; two hyper simple names given to two extraordinarily deep and complex collections of wildly sporadic and difficult to navigate- or even quantify- philosophical concepts. Political discourse proving often difficult, and abrasive, the task of narrowing it has been subsequently monopolised almost in its entirety by the media, who not only present their own narratives, but ideologically driven as they are, act as a megaphone for politicians to present theirs.

The Persistent Influence of The Media.

The media is an informational banking sector, collectively selling us suspect and poorly explained ideological PPI. Discussion of subjects such as politics and religion has been distilled into a volatile dichotomy of agreement and disagreement. We are at the point now, and perhaps have been for longer than we think (in which case we really ought to have learned by now), whereby so much discussion is presented as "you either agree or you're wrong". Talking to people about politics is dangerous not because there isn't any fruit left to harvest from political discussion, or because political discussion is damned to always be chronically boring, but because political discussion has been rendered uniquely toxic. And such a desperate shame it is.

Tommy Robinson. Upon even seeing that name, some people reading will likely be rolling their eyes and wondering why I even bothered mentioning it. He's a racist thug, right? The founder of an ultra alt right organisation hell bent on murdering Muslims and blacks? And if we are honest, probably Jews, right? Okay, but I have one question: Why? Where precisely has this perception come from? People will often call him stupid. Based on what? The man has written two books. Trust me when I say that is not an easy or simple feat. He is extraordinarily well read and well versed on what it is that concerns him- namely Islam and the cultural erosion of the UK- because in no small part of the necessity in becoming so well versed to even begin tackling a problem like that. If you are of the persuasion of thinking that hates Tommy Robinson- generally if you always refer to him as "Stephen Yaxley- Lennon" you fall into that category- then where has your information come from? More pressingly, how has that perception been shaped? And be honest now, because if your opinions of Tommy Robinson have been shaped by what the BBC, the Independent, the Mirror and the Guardian have to say, and even still by the fact that you already dislike any publications you have seen defend him (and there are so very few it's hard to find an example), then you aren't as enlightened as I fear you might think.

In the interest of balance, the same thing can be said for anyone who describes Jeremy Corbyn as a "Marxist", not least because even amongst serious academics, Marxism is extremely hard to define and inconsistently used to reference various (and sometimes conflicting) ideological positions. So, what do you specifically mean? That he supports economic redistribution? Atheism? Secularism? How do they make him a Marxist? Does he seek to abolish wealth or simply redistribute it, and to what extent? What even is it to be a Marxist anyway- almost none of them would *necessarily* see Corbyn as one of their own, so what are we really saying when we call Corbyn a Marxist? These questions are not arbitrary, either; they are not inconsequential. The nuances behind what is meant by what we say *have* to matter, and do matter, and yet we so seldom as a population give them a second consideration.

This is no accident. This is a marvel of intellectual engineering, and it relies upon a broad foundation of ignorance. For it is upon that foundation that the media can build those ever-dangerous narratives we explored all those pages and chapters ago. The media, safe in the knowledge that it controls the information we receive as well as how we receive it and as such how we interpret it, is free to develop those narratives and spin an ever more complex web of misunderstandings, assumptions, axioms and presumptions. On top of this, when the media bands together by ideological faction and the left join in spinning the same web, and the right in spinning their own, the message is not only made louder and echoed ever further, but is gently accepted by the broadly ignorant and ratified in credibility. It is also within the media, and within this principle, where conversation is most limited and the rules governing the aforementioned perceptions we develop are written.

One of the strangest fallouts from this ideological media monopoly is that because of the toxicity surrounding political discussion, we will not discuss our disagreements and if we do, such discussions almost certainly turn very heated and quite nasty in little time. Repetitive, predictable media soundbites from all angles create a cacophony of argument and political noise that is often little more than misjudged irreverence, except from in the very rare case. Herein lies the reason that this equates in my mind to "ideological PPI"; misinformation sold to us by media outlets benefits them tremendously, in terms of sales, exposure and public awareness, and is often met with almost inconsequential punishment, such as the Sun newspaper having to issue but an arbitrary apology for a "significantly misleading" article suggesting one in five British Muslims sympathised with Jihadis[56]. The consequences of the media's actions are always far outweighed by the benefits, in an emphatic ode to the banks and PPI.

What this does first and foremost is insulate opinions from the magic and critique of constructive, intellectually driven discourse. Playing by the rules presented by the media approach to ideological discussion, and assuming a position according to which ever ideological position they most identify with, people are often rendered unwilling to fail and more frustratingly unwilling to be incorrect, even at a fundamental ideological level- calling Corbyn a Marxist, for example, is irresponsible and misguided, not least because realistically, we would never find ourselves comrades of a Marxist state under him. In practice this just speaks to a shortfall in people's education on the nuances and intricate differences between Marxism and the various iterations of socialism, and allows the monopoly on that education to fall ever tighter into the grasp of the ideological mis-sellers of the media.

A losing battle, which we never fought.

Everywhere that we are exposed to politics, ideology, opinions and politicians, there is an agenda; a pre-conceived intention of what *ought to* be interpreted by what is being conveyed. Discussion often becomes argument, and whilst the fire of argument *can* be useful in exploring subjects and reaching a state of enlightenment, there are very few platforms upon which, going about our daily lives, we can actually have a productive discussion or argument, especially over something such as politics where we ardently and entirely disagree with the opposing party. It might have been fair to presume that the advent of social media would have fixed this problem. We can now be fairly certain that it has done the polar opposite.

---

[56] Available here: <https://www.bbc.co.uk/news/uk-35903066>

It simply doesn't happen, and people *en masse* are not accustomed to the art of argument, the intellectual dance that is the heated back and forth of dogmatic positions. They are accustomed to having an opinion and doing their best to prove its validity. Droll and banal as that assessment may be, in my experience and in observable social interactions, it unfortunately holds true. People are not looking to explore subjects or refine and craft their opinions, they are looking to bolster them. This delightful terminology rearing its head once again, they solicit their own ignorance by virtue of already having made up their minds. The psychologists of the world may refer to this phenomenon as "confirmation bias".

The power of this ignorance can extend far beyond academic debate or subject exploration. The idea of a kind of instinctive morality, where by it is presumed that what we think is right, *is* absolutely and objectively right, and applicable to everyone (part of the reason the West got so carelessly involved in the middle East) is a damning example of how broad and deep this philosophical, ideological and political ignorance can go. For all the philosophical turmoil associated with this broken line of thinking, considering that morality and moral standards being for millennia at the epicentre of human conversation and contemplation, this ignorance is made all the worse, and truly highlights the lack of broad social development in the fields of thought this book is concerned with.

We all so often subscribe to the notion that there is an accepted morality amongst the west, ground our political beliefs in a completely uncritiqued version of this morality, and vehemently argue our politics on that basis. Morality has evolved within the perceptions of the modern electorate, and this is a phenomenon political parties are more than privy to; it is in fact something they actively encourage, like an intellectual sheep dog rounding up the ideological herd. With the evolution of morality comes the evolution of what is socially and politically acceptable, and it is thus used as a basis for manifesto building by political parties. The Conservative party, for example, has distanced itself markedly from a position even remotely resembling one of ideological conviction in favour of the profitable morality politics developed by various iterations of Liberalism over the last 30 years. Having a multi-point manifesto and a complex set of goals is difficult, and articulating the philosophy behind all those individual factors is a difficult ad unforgiving task. As such, it was a task that exhausted itself in the Thatcher years and never really recovered since. You can now separate the manifestos of the major political parties with a cigarette paper, as has been the case for decades. Sure, the wording they use makes them seem markedly different, but remember that the 2019 manifesto of the conservatives was one promising masses of spending (including over

£5bn for broadband[57], which if anything like the catastrophe that has been HS2 will no doubt near Jeremy Corbyn's £20bn broadband pledge[58] by the time it has been rolled out), and the budget presented by Rishi Sunak[59]- after infamous Thatcherite Sajid Javid was sacked for disagreements with economic policy- in early 2020 was one which decimated any argument whatsoever that the Conservatives used to have about economic robustness.

Far from advocating a small state and explaining it or shifting the discourse to a decidedly conservative social tonality, the rise of soft, morality politics has made headway, and revealed firstly the political revenue to be raised by feeding such morality centric rhetoric, and secondly, that intricate explanation of ideology isn't necessary when all they are *really* trying to do is get elected. This was shown to be nothing but misguided effort to repackage socialist ideology throughout the unsuccessful Labour campaigns of the '80s, and in the failure of the lacklustre John Major in the 90s. However, the true master of moral politicking was Blair, and it was under Blair that it reached its apex. Blairs neo-liberal- pseudo- socialist, Frankenstein's monster hybrid of political ideology was sold as having moral virtue, goodness and kindness at its heart, whilst maintaining the tried and tested economics of Thatcher and the ruse of sensibility in its brain. His all-encompassing "Big Tent" would ensure that nobody had to suffer the plight of being an under achiever, or be held accountable for their own failure. It was to insulate us from the nastiness of competitive achievement and the disparity between those that can and those that won't. The genius of Tony Blairs Big Tent was that it began the profound process of removing competitiveness from the social psyche.

Though the statistics (in all their irreverent glory) highlight this point[60], they're unnecessary because it was a memorable, and tangible, phenomenon-

---

57 A questionable £5bn at that: < https://www.bbc.co.uk/news/technology-49881168>

58 Available here: <https://www.theguardian.com/technology/2019/nov/18/jeremy-corbyns-broadband-plan-how-it-differs-from-australias-nbn-the-blunder-down-under> Corbyn came under artillery fire for his commitment to the pledge, but it wasn't quite clear as to why aside from the tired and clearly disingenuous rhetoric used by the Tories of "magic money trees" etc. Clearly partisan, clearly engineered to appeal to the media moulded political ignorance of the masses, clearly an attempt to mask their own inadequacy.

59 Analysed here in all its Keynesian, interventionist, pseudo redistributive glory: <https://www.bbc.co.uk/news/uk-politics-51850740>

60 IFS spending figures for Labour governments up to 2010 <https://www.ifs.org.uk/bns/bn92.pdf>

the explosion of social welfare and benefits recipients, the money being thrown into everything, the increased funding for schools, the money thrown at the NHS (and yes, we spend more comparatively now as the Tories would stringently attest, a testament to the legacy of the Blairite contribution to liberalism and their subscription to its doctrine), the amount of public parks being built. Money was everywhere, and everywhere was insulated from the ideological poison seeping in because they were wrapped in a rose scented blanket of postmodern liberal moral righteousness.

This philosophical ignorance persists and provides an interesting conclusive window as to the extent of our ignorance, having already established its power: we, as a population, really have little idea when it comes to ideological philosophy, let alone how it translates into politics, and for this reason it so often manifests itself in animosity and fear. Humans always fear the unknown. This assertion may at first strike the reader as perhaps grotesquely broad brush, or even horrifically arrogant, but consider the following: upon asking a fully grown adult to address the verb in the sentence "the cat sat on the mat" I would suggest that even after years of English education, and years of language mastery, many would hesitate, with a fair percentage being unable to answer without guessing; the same goes for asking them to outline a determiner or a noun in the same sentence. Many would struggle, and this is regarding a subject we have all had years of stringent education on, at every level of our academic lives. Now, ask your average adult in the UK to discuss utilitarianism, explain who Jeremy Bentham is, the significance of Edmund Burke to modern conservatism, why Jean Jacques Rousseau was an important influence on the French revolution, the evolution of liberalism and its foundations, or even something so straight forward to the political academic as quantifying the differences between rationalism and empiricism, and you won't be met with guess work, you will likely be met with nothingness.

Most people have never been exposed to these ideas, and are often never educated on them, and yet their opinions find their way into all avenues of political commentary. Granted, as this account has outlined, anecdotal, subjective evidence can and does certainly produce fruit within political discourse, but the fruit it produces isn't necessarily ripe without the proper intellectual nutrition. The likes of Burke and Nietzsche held that elitism was not a bad thing, in almost any context, but particularly in matters of socio-political philosophical discussion, and I am inclined to agree with them.

In the same vain as I have no place commenting on the advancement of bioluminescent trees, or the investigation of the properties of dark matter, because I am ignorant to the intricacies, foundations and even the implications of those fields of study, so too are people that haven't been educated properly on philosophy and politics ignorant, and broadly unqualified to comment if we apply the same rules and standards as we would with any other specialised subject. Do not mistake my sentiments here and assume I am saying that people have no *right* to comment on politics or philosophy; they absolutely do, and macro level political discussion is something we need more of, not less. What I am saying, however, is that they have been *robbed* of the ability to do so in a consistently fruitful way because of the failings of a society that has seemingly forgotten the value of these things and has even systematically sought to reduce peoples' intelligence in these areas.

For the postmodern liberal, it serves a great many purposes to not only shift the definition of what is socially intellectually desirable away from anything which could encourage the scrutiny of the ideological system they are trying to impose with a view to wielding power, but also it serves to limit what little commentary and discussion there is around these subjects to a select few minds and a very narrow pool of contribution. It is always better to make bets on cards you have dealt from a deck you shuffled yourself, especially when playing against a group of blind men.

X
The Pursuit of
Understanding.

"Any fool can know. The point is to understand."- Albert Einstein

The general tonality throughout this book may well seem- or even be- unclear, not least in the fact that it may not be immediately self-evident whether it is a critique of ideology, stubbornness, philosophy, the general populous, politics, politicians- or even something else. For me, as your sometimes-humble author, that would be perfection; it is not supposed to be clear, precisely because it is a matter of subjective understanding and interpretation as to what it will mean, to *you*. It is a book exploring the transformation of thoughts into policy; of philosophy into power. It is a book exploring the curious and often self-imposed limitations we place on our own thought and consideration, and a book positing questions which try to encourage a deviation from one's own dogma. There is a catastrophic trajectory of modern thinking- modern philosophy and modern ideology- that will undoubtedly lead us to a place where we will invariably find misery being sold as progress, the decimation of individual autonomy sold to us as freedom, and an economy of virtue paid for with the currency of intellectual conformity.

Philosophy, ideology, politics and power are fractured concepts, almost impossible to understand in their own right- or more specifically, almost impossible to quantify as homogenous concepts- and as such are always destined to be a matter of ongoing and infinite human discussion. There will never be uniform agreement within any of these concepts; a bold claim maybe, but here we are in the 21st century with no uniform agreement on such seemingly simple concepts as what gender is or even if the planet Earth is flat.

Why then, do politics and philosophy command so much attention in our lives? Why do we work so hard to involve ourselves with a subject in which we are so poorly equipped to engage? Why are these things so factional, so abrasive and divisive, so infuriating and emotive? It is because of exactly the same thing that attracted every philosopher to the subject of philosophy in the first place: pure, brilliant, human curiosity. People are curious, naturally. We have an affinity for the question "why?", and it manifests itself so beautifully in the guise of political argument, because to the layperson philosophy is discussed best in a seemingly political context and, in a similar but lesser vain, a simple ideological context, based on the unique ability for politics and simplified ideology to deliver and articulate philosophy and philosophical positions, and to quantify philosophical thought and morality through political parties and the policies they produce. Hence the discourse on the right labelling liberals (social/ progressive liberals specifically but blanket terminology isn't a concern for most of these would be commentators) as weak, is testimony to their philosophy of strength, meritocracy, equality of opportunity, an at best catchment welfare state, a free market and the value of competition compared with the (social) liberal's reverence of paternalist welfare, equality of outcome, redistribution of wealth, wealth's perceived asphyxiation of ambition, and the idea that an acceptable minimum quality of life should exist.

How the "conservative" (again, broadly mis used in social discussion) and "liberal" (ditto) dichotomy of politics has developed in the hyper pronounced way we are now accustomed to seeing them over the last five years or so, is a testament to people's inquisitive enthusiasm but lacking knowledge of their causes. The two factions of "conservative" and "liberal", like to a lesser extent political parties, have become ideological way posts, identity markers that allow for the broad bringing together of topics and themes which broad cohorts of people *tend* to agree with, and within them contain *general* characteristics that help to identify and define people's individual morality.

In essence, over simple quantification of ideology and philosophy into these two factions, and then a fragmentation thereof into political parties, is useful because it reduces extraordinarily complex theories and concepts down into easily understandable and digestible soundbites. It also highlights two important principles: firstly, that people, in general, want what they think is best for themselves and naturally suppose that what is best for themselves is best for society, and that secondly, politics are often approached in an adversarial way much in the same way as sports teams. If you align with a certain way of thinking then it is only natural to assume opposing thinkers have been "conditioned", or stumbled erroneously, into thinking that their way is better, and therefore it is up to you to prove them wrong.

There is almost *always* a subjective grandeur of one's own opinion, which is almost always accompanied by bewilderment that others will not receive your argument or reasoning. In the empirical sciences[61], hypotheses, figures, numbers and facts can quickly negate such conflicts, as one can literally *observe* the fact that water is a compound made of hydrogen and oxygen, or that an atom may vibrate with such precise regularity it can be used structure the building of a clock. But with political ideas- with philosophy- which are both almost entirely rationalist disciplines depending entirely on your own adopted logic and rationale, your own mind is master, and one's own reasoning, interpretation and meaning is individual, unique and sovereign. I could look at exactly the same Trussell trust figures on food bank usage as you and yet draw (and defend) completely different conclusions. Society as an idea, morality and philosophy are entirely in the eye of the beholder, fathomed usually from said beholder's unique compilation of life experiences, both mental and physical; manifestations of their mydeology.

Philosophy.

Philosophy, at its core, is reference to the process of thinking and consideration. Philosophers are such not because they have compelling answers to intricate questions, but because they ask the intricate questions, often knowing that that the answer is probably beyond them. To philosophise is to think, but not in the same mindless way as watching a soap opera on the TV or operating a till requires; to philosophize is to think deeply and broadly about something- anything- and to seriously interrogate not just that thing, but your

---

61 Understood as Biology, Chemistry and Physics, because of their extremely structured, meticulously defined and broadly universally accepted parameters of understanding.

convictions of knowledge surrounding it. It can be the consideration of something so banal as a cup, or something so mind-blowingly intricate as the origin of the universe and the nature of what it means to exist. In some ways, the nature of the cup and the nature of all existence are of the same complexity. To think about that complexity is to philosophise.

Philosophy as thought and consideration is different to your philosophy, philosophy understood as something we possess; and we do, indeed, all possess a philosophy. "Your philosophy" is the culmination of all the decisions you have made as to your positions on everything from the spiritual to the moral. Your philosophy is the collection of that which has been deeply considered enough by you to be categorised as important. Your philosophy is your morality, your ideology and your actions. Your philosophy is the story of your sentient development as a human being, as prestigious as that honour is. Your philosophy is unique to you, because only you have had precisely the life, influences and experiences that you have had. Your philosophy becomes the blueprint for your internal, raw, ambiguous ideology; your mydeology.

The ambiguity of ideology is perhaps its most dangerous and also its most critical characteristic, because it is a symptom of the broadness of thought across all of humanity. It is often intentionally overlooked because with ambiguity comes inconsistency, and a much more fractured pluralism of ideological categorisation- it serves a great many purposes to whittle the ideological dialogue down to two ostensibly straight forward teams. "Conservative or Liberal", as the west increasingly has it, is a much easier, simpler contrast around which to conduct the business of argument, than one involving all the nuanced philosophical positions of the populous or the confusing cacophonous voices of the many splinter ideologies such as classical liberals, postmodern liberals, social liberals, anarcho-conservatives, one nation conservatives, Thatcherite conservatives, Burkean conservatives, neo conservatives and all the rest.

It can become overwhelming and ultimately unproductive to fill discourse with ideological white noise, and it makes discussions of things so important and complex as that of right and wrong much more difficult to have. If personal philosophies are what attract us towards an ideology, then it is easier and more broadly productive to limit political leaning, as far as possible, to one of two sides. In limiting this, however, what we are tacitly doing is limiting discourse and discussion, obliging it to fit into one of these broad and inconsistently defined oceans of philosophical meaning- and that is what the ideological categories of "conservative" and "liberal" are at their very core: oceans of philosophical meaning.

Oceans of philosophical meaning are places within which ideas are distorted, morality is crafted, and broad decisions are made as to why the world should exist in the way you suppose it should. Ideologies are so much larger than politics- they are aggregates of mydeologies, of everything it is to be an individual, everything individual minds believe and consider, everything they think makes them human and differentiates them from beast. In a facetious and extremely crude way, I suppose you could perhaps even define whatever it is that governs the actions of animals and beasts as their philosophy; the very fact they *do* things by definition implies that they *think* things. Their lacking ability to explain and quantify those philosophies, as well as translate them into ideological categories, branches and factions, is perhaps what most makes them beastly; or maybe having that ability is what makes us beastly.

The advanced interpretations of how humans value morality, society (as an idea), and philosophy, are, however, not just aggregate interpretations of "the way things should be" or a collection of moral positions; they are developed by, and symptomatic of, many other things. Any number of subjective experiential interpretations can trigger emotions, such as jealousy, hatred, envy, happiness, joy or others, and affect not just *what* we value, but also *why* we value it. These emotions are crucial to our interpretations which produce the very reasoning that is critical in guiding how we value things. Philosophies in that regard are products of emotion, at their core. It is fine to sit here and suggest that our minds are captured by media villains and political playwrights, doing all they can to engross us in a drama in which they are the lead actors and we are the talentless spectators mindlessly cheering and jeering them on, but that would be to sell short the very essence of what any thought truly is: the process of the individual self-actualising, and manifesting their emotions in expression. Ideologies just give these thoughts relevance and weight beyond the self.

If something makes you happy, usually it is something to be actively sought out, and is often qualified in your mind as being something "good". Happiness then begins to become synonymous with good. If something, conversely, makes you sad, it is often qualified as being "bad". Sadness is tantamount to badness. Therefore, the relationship between the paradigms of "happy/ sad" and "good/ bad" is one upon which the basis of moral judgments can be inferred, and if moral judgements can be inferred, they can be manipulated; ideologies can begin to take shape. Here we hopefully begin to spin the web of how ideology develops, as well as the influencing factors which contribute to that development. Our proclivity to equate happiness to good and sadness to bad does not by any means suggest that the defining quality of all that is either good or bad relates to happy and sad, but it does act as a reliable barometer to guide our morality and as such, produces rhetoric within which ideologies can ensnare us.

Emotions are important, because they dictate our reactions to situations. If you feel like you are ugly, you will change some aspect of your life accordingly; not necessarily for the better, but it will affect you, and you will react to the emotion that the feeling inspires. Perhaps, for example, you will become more reserved, more bitter or more frustrated with life. Perhaps you will think about ways in which you can make yourself less ugly, or even not ugly at all, and implement them to improve your situation. Perhaps; perhaps not.

Emotions and expression are inextricably linked, as are to a similar degree expression and action. To express oneself, first one must feel; for, if you do not feel, what is there even to express and, more pressingly, why would you express it? Action is therefore always a form of expression, and it is also as such always commissioned by feeling. Action is expression commissioned by emotion, and emotion is the essence of thought. All this is important because emotions shape our perspectives on the world, and our perspectives shape our philosophies, which eventually develop into our ideological allegiances. In this way the ideologies we choose to identify with and follow are extensions of ourselves, and way markers along the road towards understanding life.

Ideology.

Our ideology is more than just a banal, single, seldom understood, hyper manufactured word. Ideologies capture our emotions, and ideology fits into the puzzle of understanding life ubiquitously. Ideology is the dictionary of our thoughts, which are, crudely, ideas that serve as solutions to problems. It is a reference book of what ideas and concepts mean, to us, understood as individuals, and how they can be applied, utilised or distributed by us as individuals. Ideology is a collation of what we deem acceptable emotional responses to certain stimuli- whether that stimuli be physical, metaphysical, metaethical or otherwise- and the culmination of our conclusions as to the usefulness and reasonability of those responses. Ideology is not politics; politics is the implementation of ideologies. Ideology by itself, of its own accord, to the individual, existing individually, is straightforwardly a reference book.

It is this ability to think, consciously, critically and provocatively, which separates man from beast; it is this which makes us quintessentially sentient. There is little to no compelling evidence that animals- beasts- deduce actions, feelings or thoughts as good or bad, right or wrong, evil or pure[62]. Morality is of no concern to animals, bound as they are to act entirely with necessity and pragmatism in mind, within the limitations of their natural ability. Democracy is of no concern to animals. Justice is of no concern to animals, at least not understood as humans understand justice. We, exclusively as sentient humans, have given names to these manifestations of action and the emotions which commission them. You cannot act unfairly to a dog; only acceptably or unacceptably. You cannot act kindly to a bear; only acceptably or unacceptably. This is because these concepts are strictly human in creation, definition and implementation. What is it to be kind? Is sharing half your food with another human generous, kind, or stupid? What do you think? Now, what would a bear think? We don't know- and we couldn't possibly- but rest assured, should you ever try taking half of a bear's food you will be considered to be acting in a wholly unacceptable way; the bear will not worry about being thought of as selfish, or acting "selfishly".

At this point, you may be wondering what the significance of bears is to this subject matter, chapter, or even this book. You may be trying to understand the point being made. You may already understand the point being made; what is important is that you have the capacity to understand the point being made. Understanding is not just the lifeblood of human conception; it is the defining factor in human intellectual supremacy. Our unique capacity to question, define, categorise and understand things is our supreme condition. It is also our interpretation of that understanding- all of that understanding, positive or negative- that eventually becomes a large deciding factor in our choosing an ideological home.

Ideology is there before it is individually quantifiable (conservative thinking was there long before it was defined as conservatism, as was Marxist or socialist thinking) and it is so much broader than banal quantifications of simply "conservative or liberal", "Nazi or fascist". The truth of the matter is that "ideologies" as we know them- any ideologies, from liberalism to communism to Nazism to egalitarianism- are broad, simplified, easy ways in which to find

---

[62] Frans De Waal writes extensively on this position, and convincingly in some ways, but an impossible hurdle he fails to negotiate in my mind is the hurdle of requiring complex language to make actual, truly *moral* judgements, because of the impossible complexity of explaining them without it. To act in a moral way requires not just the capacity, but the propensity to act in a certain way *knowing* that acting in another way might benefit you more. To understand this and to present these problems is a matter of language and philology, not simple observations and correlations.

philosophical common ground, and in doing so find the support and affirmation we all lust after. Psychologically speaking, to find one of our "in groups" and identify more easily our "out groups". They are namesakes given to clusters of conceptual positions.

Consider this: All closed shapes with three sides are triangles, but if all these sides are of equal length then that definition becomes more focused, into "equilateral triangles". Even still, all equilateral triangles are by no means the same; they differ in area, size, material- several different qualities. Is a field in the precise shape of an equilateral triangle the exact same as a lake in the precise shape of an equilateral triangle? If not, are the differences between the two worth fighting- or dying- for? Perhaps not, but in ideology, these variances may well be worth that sacrifice, and the difference between what you believe to be right and wrong in contrast to what someone else may believe to be right or wrong can be that nuanced. Ideologies, as we have constructed and usually understand them, appropriate concepts and ideas for their own definition, allowing us to broadly categorise things in a broadly accurate way, and progress from there with that as our understanding henceforth. This understanding, like that of triangles, might appear rigid at first glance, but it is decidedly fluid in reality.

Thusly, the primary reason that we as individuals develop an ideology is because of one finite concept: understanding. Fredrich Nietzsche very famously (or infamously) wrote a magnificent polemic named "The Will to Power"[63] in which he alludes to all living creatures' constant and primal pursuit of power, their lust for expanding that power, and the fight in which they all participate to establish their dominance within their species and within the entirety of the animal kingdom. For most animals, power translates into how much food they have, how much territory they control, the size of their pack or "group", the strength of their group and how easily, in essence, they can survive. For humans, it is slightly different, and the will to power is not so simple as satisfying hunger, being strong, finding shelter and having sex. We do quite a good job of survival, at least in the west, by default now. We as a species have surpassed that banal necessity.

For us, power must manifest itself in other ways- in violence, in politics, in the exercise of choice, in self-mastery, in capital (monetary and otherwise)- all of which rely entirely upon one thing: an *understanding* of knowledge. To accrue any of the above, we must understand our ability to do it, our capacity to

63 Nietzsche, F., Hill, R., Scarpitti, M. and Nietzsche, F. (n.d.). *The will to power.*

do it, the scenarios within which they would be useful and the scenarios where it would be proper to use them. Knowing we *can* is not the same as understanding *when and how* we should. Understanding is the critical factor of life, if life is indeed about the will to power, which it seems to me is most certainly the case. Understanding is the critical factor for life if it is about happiness, understood (extraordinarily simplistically) in terms of maximizing "good" feelings and minimizing "bad". Understanding is the critical factor of life if you want to join the rat race, get the 9-5 job, 2.4 kids and two cars. Understanding is the critical factor of life even if you *don't* want to play the game; you have to understand what you *don't* want just as much as you have to understand what you *do* want. Understanding is the critical factor of life if you want to be happy, sad, strong, weak, charming, rich, poor, fulfilled, empty, loved or hated. If understanding is power, and power is something we ought to tacitly pursue, then ideology is our beacon of light through the dark abyss that is existence and thought without meaning. Perhaps a life without ideology is nihilism, just as the colour black is in fact just the complete absence of light.

This definition of power is different in some ways for humans than the definition for beasts; in other ways, not so much, and the principle way in which the two remain similar is that generally speaking, power is magnified with numbers. In many ways, power is a numbers game, and the concept of ideology thrives on this fact. We are incentivised to identify and proliferate ideologies because of this fact, and because of the nature of human politics. Ideologies remove the stress and pressure of decision making from the individual and allow the individual to outsource their philosophical autonomy to a common focus point. Instead of having to confront the difficult philosophical questions presented so regularly in daily life and to handle them yourself, offering the very time-consuming thought and perilous consideration they all require in some capacity, you can relegate philosophical autonomy to your ideology and reference it directly when these problems arise. This is perhaps the most important revelation when exploring what an "ideology" actually is and the purpose they serve: the revelation that ideologies blur the line between individual philosophy and that of the collective, not least because even "individualistic" ideologies are followed by multiple individuals, and become *de facto* collectives. In fact, they can perhaps be quite fairly defined as aggregate philosophies; philosophical collectives.

Viewing them in this way guides us towards a profound benefit of combining your philosophical positions into an ideology: that they give the individual purpose beyond the self. They not only allow for the acquisition of power, in accordance with Nietzsche's doctrine, and the relegation of the effort it takes to seriously and deeply think about moral positions and political phenomenon to the ideological group, but they also give you metaphysical companions, friends; easily identifiable like minds. Ideologies not only have the quality of proving that you're not alone (because naturally, for something to be an ideology it has to be recognised by more than one person), but they have the unparalleled scope to unionise minds behind similar principles in the pursuit of further power; usually, but not always, political power. At the personal, individual level, philosophy metamorphosising into ideology gives you not just something to fight for, but *someone* to fight for, beyond the self. Ideologies use your philosophical positions and conclusions to straightforwardly offer you both purpose and reason, and that is not to say nothing; purpose and reason are extraordinarily profound intellectual gifts.

Power.

These gifts are useful, and to most people extremely valuable. Anything of value is worth paying for, and this principle is the first way in which ideology becomes about the acquisition and transfer of power. Power is a curious mistress, and it is ultimately the concept which attracts the hungry mind to the nutrition of ideology. Ideology is in many ways the end product of our socialisation. When we engage with life in any way, shape or form, in any sensory context, we engage with ideological development. All of our individual experiences (not just of feelings, but also of things) inspire within us some ideological leaning- some qualities of a quantifiable philosophical form- and allow, eventually, for the sure categorisation of those qualities into their ideological shape. This is to say that firstly, all ideologies as they are understood have been categorised by man for the sake of accessible discussion, scrutiny and interrogation, and that secondly, ideologies are all generalisations; ideologies by their very nature are imprecise, to allow for movement, change, development, growth and expansion.

Ideology is a supremely flexible principle and it is as such no surprise that one can describe a spectrum of "conservative philosophers" and a spectrum of "liberal philosophers" and yet also seemingly describe the specific ideology of "conservatism" or "liberalism". Ideologies are a vehicle upon which we can navigate through the world on a path of understanding best suited to our desired goals- if, for example, you want things like equity, the removal of wealth inequality, common ownership of industry and broad population representation in the political process, then socialism may well be an appropriate vehicle with which to navigate that journey, but even then, that isn't to say that there is only one road.

Power at its very core for humans is understanding. Understanding is what gives the individual, in any situation, the ability to live and thrive or condemns them to failure. In the pursuit of this understanding we as individual often conflict, clash and challenge one another. Similarly, if the one over which you wish to have dominion does not understand why you are powerful, it is unlikely they will capitulate to your demands, and more to the point, logically speaking, why would they? When we pursue this understanding, we run into hurdles and sometimes have to stumble and fall, stop and regroup, reassess and re-evaluate.

This process of exploring ideas is of itself empowering, in so far as it reveals to us more of the self, in an unavoidably honest way. When our understanding falls short, or reveals to us cracks in our intellectual armour, we are forced into a position whereby we either have to actively choose ignorance or the more difficult position of admitting that we are wrong. Ideology offers this lesson of understanding in a myriad of ways, and they are not all -or even mostly- bad or odious. For example, it offers us the chance to interrogate how ideas become things, and to interrogate the things that ideas become. Why, for example, did we go to war with Iraq? What specifically led up to the invasion of Iraq, the overthrowing of Saddam Hussein and the destabilisation of the Middle East? The banal, obvious choice of reasoning is the idea that Hussein was a "tyrant" and that there was supposed evidence of weapons of "mass destruction". Maybe, but what is the problem with tyranny? Many a layperson and academic alike have deeply pondered these questions, and it is right that they have done so. Whether any definitive answer can or will ever be found is irrelevant; the point is that the interrogation is there, and the opportunity for greater understanding thusly ever present.

Ideology can be understood, conclusively, in two ways (although it is almost always expressed on the premise of the first): firstly, as a namesake given to a quantifiable collection of standardised and recognised social, moral and political positions, or secondly, as the collection of every and all social, moral and political positions we hold as an individual, in their collective entirety; that which this account has called a "mydeology". The problem with the first is that we have to assimilate; we are captive to the crowd and the group think that invariably comes with it. The problem with the second is that by definition, it is not shared by anyone.

Our mydeology is absolutely and completely unique to us all. It will inevitably fall in line with broader categories of ideological quantification, and invariably always does, but it is never even close to identical to that of any other individual. As our perceptions of ideology and how to categorise and discuss it have diversified and broadened throughout history, so too, oxymoronically, have they become increasingly narrow and in many ways limited. We all have a mydeology, we are all a unique cacophony of ideas that have manifested themselves in an individual mind. Some are similar; none are the same. We are all in the pursuit of understanding who we are, what we want, why we want it and how we can possibly go about achieving or attaining these things.

It is within this concept that the true power of ideology is realised. Whether it be the individual realising their potential and capacity for success, a collective group intellectually unionising to forward their agenda, a political party weaponising the presumption that we want and pursue understanding, or an employee looking to work their way up the corporate ladder, ideology is and always will be a stepping stone to power.

Humanity seeks power. The beauty of ideology lies in its capacity, as a concept at the broader level and a reality at the more narrow "mydeological" level, to offer ways of achieving power with which the powerless will be (and remain) complicit. Political parties overtly use collectivist ideologies for power and make no bones about embracing the aforementioned understanding of the utility of ideology in doing that. Individuals utilise this principle differently, however. They use their mydeology to formulate and manipulate relationships and interactions, using their developed emotional reference book that is their mydeology to temper their behaviour and to maximise benefit to them. This is the power of ideology and this is the goal of philosophy: to improve your life. For this reason, ideology works on multiple levels to grant and distribute power: personal, social and political.

At the personal level, ideology (understood best at this level as your mydeology) organises your thoughts and contextualises them. It governs how and why you should react to a stimulus, and helps you identify opportunities to gain power. At the societal level, philosophy is homogenised into a shared ideology- a culture- and allows for groups of individuals to coexist and interact with an implied set of standardised rules. Ideology at the societal level gives us the capacity to enter into a dangerous environment- an environment of driven individuals with competing interests and finite resources- and not only survive, but the capacity to be complacent and to thrive. No other known existing organic being past or present has been able to achieve the level of inter-cooperation that human beings have achieved, and the success of this ability empowers us to thrive, create bigger, broader goals, and work together to achieve them. The shared collective ideology that is a culture grants the power to a society to structure and organise itself into peaceful and often beneficial hierarchical structures.

Lastly, and more anomalously, we have the political sphere of ideological distribution and power. Ideology, as we have established, ought to not be envisioned as a purely political invention. Politics is the arbitrator of competing ways of doing things, clashes of ideology. Without intellectual competition, there is no need for any conflict or disagreement, because everyone would have all the same solutions to the same problems. Ideologies exist before politics; there would be no politics without ideology. But perhaps the most potent dispersal of power granted by the concept of an ideology is visible in the imperative, unique and critical necessity that all things political have for the ideological. Politics does not exist without ideology, which means, crucially, that politicians do not exist without ideology.

To a politician, and in politics, ideology is a guide, or a map; something which people can look at and establish not just a goal or a destination, but also a path to arriving there. To a politician, the saliency, clarity and legibility of their plan is the difference between power and failure. Politicians therefore seek to manipulate and metastasise ideology- to weaponise it- in order to gain support. The necessity of ideology here forces politicians into a peculiar situation as well: they have to capture, harness, and temper emotion, because there is indeed such a thing as too much support. In politics, ideology is as volatile as it is powerful, and this forces people into situations they otherwise wouldn't need to be in. For example, when making a decision a politician (at least in a democracy) has to consider how that decision might *look* to their supporters and like-minded thinkers. They have to negotiate the perilous terrain of the minefield that is human sensitivity, without losing focus of their goals or sacrificing any power.

To these ends, we arrive at the final dimension of power to the politician: the "us" and "them" dichotomy. If you want to give people a hard pill to swallow and make them swallow it, you have to use coercion or force. Necessity is a good motivator, and if swallowing a hard pill means that "we" will win and "they" will lose, then oftentimes, so be it. Seemingly the easiest way to create a unified "us" and a clear "them" is to utilise the language of ideology.

Translating philosophy into an ideology is pointless if that ideology has no goal. Philosophy is wandering thought through an abyss of consideration; ideology is an on rails locomotive steaming towards some established and visible destination. By definition, that goal always involves power in some iteration. Ideology refines your scattered and seemingly unrelated moral standards and political positions into something resembling a plan; something with an at least theoretically achievable end goal, something with a seemingly clear path to that goal, and something offering guidance in times of doubt. Ideologies are not there to answer questions, they are there to provide stability and uniformity to the hyper complex realm of thinking and thoughts. Tribal beings as we are, we always tend towards tribalism, and ideology is nothing more than intellectual tribalism.

Understanding the Self.

What does any of this have to do with anything? Why should we think about things so deeply that it can send us insane? Why find people that share these thoughts and unionise together into an ideology? Why have a scale to define and quantify thinking at all? And why be so potent in your defence of your own ideology, and so vicious in attacking those of others? What does ideology even serve to achieve? The questions surrounding our thoughts and ideology are truly endless. That, and they also tend to be broadly subjective, which means that definitive answers to many of these questions are next to impossible to find. But perhaps it isn't answers we are trying to find, and maybe that misconception is the biggest mistake we make when looking at philosophy and ideology; their primary purpose is not to answer questions, but of their own accord, to give purpose.

Religion, as Jordan Peterson convincingly explores in *Maps of Meaning,* is of value in a multitude of ways, but most prevalently for me, it is of value because of its ability as a concept to answer impossible questions. Questions of existence, questions of purpose, questions of mind-blowing metaphysical exploration. Largely, religion does this through the medium of extraordinarily well written stories which generally have metaphorical meaning. It is magnificent for that reason alone, and Nietzsche was right to mourn the death of God. Ideologies operate much the same way, if at a lower philosophical tier. If religions answer metaphysical, existential questions, then ideologies answer more immediate questions of cooperation and morality.

And ultimately, that is what ideologies are for. They are there to answer questions and offer solutions to the problems we encounter when living with other sentient individuals who have competing interests to our own. They are there to give value to our thoughts, prescribe worth to them and, in some ways, validate them. It is for these reasons also that we hold ideologies so dear, so tenaciously fight for and defend the one to which we subscribe, and so viciously attack the ones we dislike.

We do this as well because we live in a state of animalistic fear. Fear of the unknown, fear of tyranny, fear of injustice, fear of loss, fear of violence; fear is the default position of our existence in many ways. We do not learn to fear things- it is our natural response to the unknown. Only once we understand things do we learn to delegate that fear appropriately and beneficially, to further our survival and focus our minds. Philosophy guides that process, ideology hones it, politics captures it. We allow this complex and intricate waltz to happen, in my mind, not because of any dishonest or sinister reasoning, but because of the beautiful pursuit we are all engaged in, the beautiful pursuit of understanding and power.

We allow for society to become fractured, for politicians to manipulate us and for the media to spin contrived narratives precisely because we do not understand everything, fear the unknown are not all powerful- nor will we ever be. It serves us to see where these metaphysical showmen will take us, because that place, wherever it may be, has the potential to help us increase our understanding, and to therefore increase our own self-mastery. We, as humans (good and bad) practice a beautiful curiosity and engage in such a wonderful show of our unique and important condition that is sentience through the mediums discussed in this book, amongst many others.

The human mind is quite possibly the most supreme, marvellous thing in all the universe; it is certainly amongst the only things in the universe to seek the understanding of itself; a concept as frightening as it is amazing. It is right that we all seek power when there is so much power to be sought, but it is no surprise that it comes with conflict, unrest, triumph and disaster. I don't think it takes much imagination to see how that principle, of itself, can be weaponised to the degree of life and death.

***

Further Reading.

This list is not a bibliography, but a selection of books which are useful for exploring the concepts of ideology and power; all books are conducive to philosophy, because all information shapes our perceptions and conceptions of phenomena.

These books are not by any means a finite list of exploration for all the concepts discussed in this book. Not even close. This list is but a snippet, a selection of steppingstones, as it were, which a curious mind could use to travel an intellectual journey.

Where that journey may lead is not something I could speculate upon; it is probably clear to you now that the author of this book leans to the right, but for this particular work there is no agenda of guiding your thought to any place in particular; just merely the virtuous intention of encouraging you to think.

- Aristotle. and Jowett, B., 2000. *Politics*. Dover Publications.

- Bartlett, J., n.d. *The People Vs Tech*.

- Buckingham, W., 2011. *The Philosophy Book*. London: DK Pub.

- Butler, J., 2006. *Gender Trouble*. Taylor and Francis.

- Foucault, M., 1977. *Discipline & Punish*. New York: Pantheon Books.

- Fukuyama, F., 2006. *The end of history and the last man: with a new afterword*. New York, Ny Free Press.

- Fukuyama, F., 2015. *Political Order And Political Decay - From The Industrial Revolution To The*. Profile Books Ltd.

***

- Fukuyama, F., 2018. *Contemporary Identity Politics And The Struggle For Recognition*. London: Profile books.

- Heywood, A., 2017. *Political Ideologies*. Basingstoke: Palgrave Macmillan.

- Heywood, A., n.d. *Political Theory*.

- Hobsbawm, E., 2011. *The Age Of Extremes*. London: Abacus.

- Kant, I., "What is Enlightenment?" (Essay) <https://www.stmarys-ca.edu/sites/default/files/attachments/files/Kant--What%20Is%20Enlightenment_.pdf>

- Legutko, R., n.d. *The Demon In Democracy*.

- Marx, K. and Engels, F., n.d. *The Communist Manifesto*.

- Marx, K., Engels, F. and Levitsky, S., 1999. *Das Kapital*. Washington, D.C: Regnery Gateway.

- McIntosh, P., *"White Privilege: Unpacking the Invisible Knapsack" <https://psychology.umbc.edu/files/2016/10/White-Privilege_McIntosh-1989.pdf>*

- McLaughlin, P. and Robinson, T., n.d. *Mohammed's Koran*.

- Murray, D., n.d. *The Madness Of Crowds*.

- Murray, D., 2017. *The Strange Death Of Liberal Europe*. London: Bloomsbury Publishing Plc.

- Niccolò Machiavelli and Goodwin, R. (2003). The prince.

- Nietzsche, F., Hill, R., Scarpitti, M. and Nietzsche, F. (n.d.). *The will to power.*.

***

- NIETZSCHE, F., 2018. *BEYOND GOOD AND EVIL*. ARCTURUS Publishing LTD.

- Nietzsche, F., 2008. *On The Genealogy Of Morals*. Oxford: Oxford University Press.

- Nozick, R., 2003. *Philosophical Explanations*. Cambridge, Mass.: Harvard University Press.

- Pagden, A., 1995. *Lords Of All The World : Ideologies Of Empire In Spain, Britain And France C.1500-C. 1800*. Yale University Press.

- Paton, H., 2008. *The Categorical Imperative*. Philadelphia: Univ. of Pennsylvania Press.

- Plato., 2007. *The Republic*. London: Penguin Books ltd. (Plato's Republic)

- Peterson, J. and Van Sciver, E., 2018. *12 Rules For Life*. UK: Allen Lane.

- Rand, A. n.d. *The Virtue Of Selfishness*.

- Robinson, T., n.d. *Enemy Of The State*.

- Tepper, J. and Hearn, D., n.d. *The Myth Of Capitalism*.

- Thatcher, M., 2003. *Statecraft*. London: HarperCollins.

- Varoufakis, Y. and Mason, P., 2015. *The Global Minotaur*. London: Zed Books.

- West, E., 2012. *What We Got Wrong About Immigration And How To Set It Right*. London: Gibson Square.

Printed in Great Britain
by Amazon